A New Age Kundalini

Tantra

Autobiography of a Love-Yogi

Premyogi Vajra

A NEW AGE KUNDALINI TANTRA~ AUTOBIOGRAPHY OF A LOVE-YOGI

First edition. February 24, 2024.

ISBN: 979-8224630837

Written by premyogi vajra.

A New Age Kundalini Tantra
Autobiography of a Love-Yogi

Author: Premyogi Vajra
2024

Book introduction~

Premyogi Vajra is a man full of spiritual mysteries. He is enlightened, and his Kundalini has also been awakened. He has attained Yoga Siddhi both naturally and also through artificial method i.e. practice of Kundalini Yoga. The author has beautifully penned down his spiritual experiences in the book. In this book, Premyogi Vajra has thrown some light on his unique spiritual and tantric experiences along with his related biography. In this, basic and simple Kundalini Yoga techniques have been described even for the curious and beginning seekers. Subtle light has been thrown on basic sex along with sociality. Premyogi Vajra has very well described his glimpse enlightenment and related situations in it. For those who want to understand the hidden psychology behind yoga, this book is no less than a boon. The basic theoretical secret of man-woman relations is also hidden in this book. If someone wants to drink the nectar of love, then there seems to be no better solution than this book. The secrets hidden behind socialism and monism have also been exposed in this book. In fact this book touches all areas. If someone wants to understand Hinduism in depth, there does not seem to be any other book like this book. Even if unfortunately one's family or social life is problematic, there seems to be no match for this book. This book is suitable and beneficial for all categories of people, from ordinary people (even the so-called over worldly and those without sadhana) to high level seekers. After reading this, the readers will definitely feel a positive change within themselves. This book is adapted from the original book titled Sharirvigyan Darshan ~ A Modern Kundalini Tantra [A Yogi's Love Story] in Hindi. Some readers said that there are many topics together in this book, hence some confusion arises. Many people don't want to read a long book, and many want to focus on a single topic. We did not consider it good to tamper with the original book, because it was written by Premyogi Vajra just after his sudden and momentary Kundalini awakening, due to which it could have some divine inspiration and divine power. That is why we have presented only the Kundalini Tantra part of it in a new form for such readers. Similarly, there is another book named Sharirvigyan Darshan, which is derived from this original book. In this, only the philosophical aspect of the body has been mainly considered. It seems that the essence and mystery of human life is hidden in this book. It is hoped that the presented book will meet the expectations of the readers.

Author Introduction~

Premyogi Vajra was born in the year 1975 in a small village situated in a beautiful basket-shape valley of Himachal Pradesh, India. He is naturally fond of writing, philosophy, spirituality, yoga, folklore, applied science and tourism. He has also done commendable work in the field of animal husbandry and veterinary medicine. He is also fond of polyhouse farming, organic farming, scientific and water-saving irrigation, rainwater harvesting, kitchen gardening, cow rearing, vermicomposting, website development, self-publishing, music (especially flute playing) and singing. He has also written around twenty books on almost all these subjects. He was also a Vedic priest for a short time, when he used to perform religious rituals in people's homes with the help of his Vedic priest grandfather. He has had some advanced spiritual experiences (enlightenment and Kundalini awakening). His autobiography including his unique experiences has been specifically shared in the book "Sharirvigyan Darshan – A Modern Kundalini Tantra (A Yogi's Love Story)" in Hindi. This book is the most important and ambitious book of his life. This book contains the life philosophy of the most important 25 years of his life. He has worked very hard for this book. Premyogi Vajra is a mysterious person. He is like an impersonator, who has no definite form of his own. Its actual form depends on the shape and form of samadhi that occurs in one's mind, no matter how it may appear from outside. He is also enlightened, and his Kundalini has also been awakened. He experienced enlightenment naturally/through Prem Yoga, and he experienced Kundalini awakening artificially/through Kundalini Yoga. At the time of natural samadhi, he got the help of symbolic or indirect Tantra Yoga, whereas at the time of artificial samadhi, he got the help of direct Tantra Yoga mostly due to the contribution of his own efforts.

Legal Disclaimer ~

This book is a kind of literature of myths/events related to spiritual-physical mixture, which is similar to spiritual Tantra Science. It has not been made by copying any pre-made literary work. Yet if it bears any resemblance to any pre-made creation, it is merely a coincidence. It is not designed to hurt any other sentiments. Readers will be responsible for any such situations arising from reading this. We are not lawyers. This book and the information contained within it are provided as an educational promotion only, and are not a substitute for any legal advice provided by your legal advisor. At the time of printing, utmost care has been taken to ensure that all the information given in this book is correct and useful for the readers, yet it is not a very deep effort. Therefore, if any kind of loss occurs due to this, the book presenter completely rejects his responsibility and accountability. Readers are responsible for their own choices, actions and their consequences. If they have any doubt regarding this, they should contact their judicial advisor.

First of all, this book is dedicated to Shri Bhole Mahadev, who is the first Guru of Tantra. Then this book is dedicated to the revered grandfather of Premyogi Vajra, Sri/Guru/the same old spiritual man, who was a great and practical karmayogi, and seemed to be the incarnation of Mahadeva, the initiator of Tantra.

Only two types of people exist in the entire cosmos. There is no difference between the two types of men, except in mental outlook. One type of man is gross, conditioned, and ignorant of the self, attached to the world and full of dual vision. On the other hand, the other type of people are subtle, free, self-aware, unattached to the world and endowed with non-dual vision. There are innumerable literature to describe the first type of man, but the description of the second type of man is found mainly in the philosophy of physiology or Sharirvigyan darshan i.e. Shavid. The gross man also tries to adopt the same approach as the subtle man, for which he takes the help of various religious and spiritual practices. However a man tries to become like them simply by observing and imitating them through Sharirvigyan darshan. In this book we will discuss the story of one such obese man. Related to this, we will discuss the life story of the subtle man in the second book related to Sharirvigyan Darshan or Shavid.

The practice of Shavid or Sharirvigyan Darshan {Physiology Philosophy} also establishes Kundalini, which can then be matured, raised up, and awakened through Hatha Yoga. Shavid also balances the upward movement of Kundalini through the paths of Ida (emotional/experiential nadi) and Pingala (abhavamay/karma nadi). Let me tell you a secret that I have experienced myself. Kundalini is actually the loveliest physical form, with its repeated practice and introduction in a friendly manner, it starts becoming stable in the mind, which is called establishment of Kundalini. Shavid fully supports free and humane life-behaviours, due to which material things start becoming mental. Yes, along with these, attention should also be paid towards Shavid. This means that one should not stop the mental tendencies and their emotions, but in between they should take a momentary and oblique glance towards the Shavid, only so that it continues as it is and there is no interference of any kind from it. This will add a touch of detachment to those behaviours and they will become pure means pure mental. One who rejects materialism does not even have mentality, because the source of mentality is materiality. If one accepts materialism or any material thing without Shavid, he will become attached to it, which will make him cling to it, instead of developing it by fixing it in its pure form in the mind. Due to this, the Kundalini will remain dependent on materiality only, in which it is not possible for its complete development.

Shavid had greatly helped Premyogi Vajra when his Kundalini had come down after the touch of enlightenment, and then had climbed up through the Ida Nadi. At that time he was mentally agitated, very sensitive, nervous, behaved like a woman, lost in divine and beautiful dreams, tired and physically weak. After mental excitement, he would suddenly sink into deep depression. During times of depression (dark state), his Kundalini was said to enter the Pingala Nadi. It was not entering both the nerves in a balanced manner, i.e. Sushumna. His physical and even mental strength had become very weak, because Kundalini used to camp in his brain with full force all the time. That Kundalini seemed more direct, alive and clear than even a living and visible human being. All the nutrition in his body was being spent in maintaining it continuously. His appetite was small and strange. Sometimes the hunger would go away, and sometimes it would increase suddenly, making it difficult to control. His working skills had also diminished, and he remained lost in solitude, mostly in the bliss of samadhi. Although spiritually these symptoms were normal, physically they were disruptive. At that time, the author, with some unknown inspiration, had published a one-page abridged version of Shavid in the university magazine. The intelligent Premyogi Vajra took inspiration from that article and created a philosophy of physiology from it. The author has merely drawn it with pen on paper. Since then, the process of thinking about Shavid had started, due to which, after about 20 years of practical and interesting efforts, this philosophy was completed. The entire Shavid was prepared from the text of that one page, just as the entire Shri Bhagwat Purana was prepared from the one verse Bhagwat. That medicine proved to be a panacea for his mental imbalance. Due to this, his Kundalini started flowing equally through both Pingala and Ida nadis and due to their opposite nature, they started balancing each other. After 20 years of hard work in the midst of a busy life, when Premyogi Vajra got 1-2 years of peaceful time with a favourable environment, he spontaneously reached an advanced stage of yoga. This means that salvation is definitely possible after a lifetime of hard work, because the last 1-2 years of life are definitely peaceful (physically or mentally or both). It is also possible that by the joint practice of Shavid and Kundalini Yoga, a man may be born on such a divine planet-constellation, where men have a spiritual mind and are themselves ready to practice yoga, to attain enlightenment easily. ; And where there is no need to use the magical tricks used on planet Earth to strengthen the brain.

It is said in Kundalini texts that 72000 nerves/nadis/channels emerge from the heart and spread throughout the body; but a nerve goes towards the brain, which leads to Brahma, that is, it leads to awakening of Kundalini. In fact, the meaning of Naadi here is intense feelings. All intense experiences are created with the help of external senses like eyes, which are said to be 72000 nadis. But the same feeling, which is also the most intense, arises only in the brain, which is depicted as that single upward pulse. The big number of 72000 is because there are countless nerve-driven sensations that we cannot perceive, but which are moving the body. For example, the innumerable nerves that run the stomach, the heart, etc.

Peace time is also relative. It is different for different people. With duality, no person can become completely hardworking. Advaita viewpoint itself leads a person to complete hard work. When a person remains completely diligent (both mentally and physically) with Advaita, then only he is called Karmayogi. With the help of Shavid, the Karmayoga of Premyogi Vajra was successful after 15-20 years of continuous effort. Although the time period may vary. Then due to some unknown motivation, if one has to change one's place of residence for 2-3 years due to migration etc., then the flow of karma of that Karmayogi gets broken. Through this he experiences a state of peace as deep as that experienced by an ordinary person when he leaves everything and takes complete renunciation. In this way, that Karma Yogi gets as great and quick results of his Kundalini Yoga Sadhana done during that short period of peace as the said Purna Sannyasi. The same incident as Karmayogi happened with Premyogi Vajra and he could experience Kundalini awakening within a year, although he had also taken shelter of sexual yoga along with Kundalini Yoga.

It is very beneficial to practice Kundalini Yoga in a peaceful state after leading a non-dual and busy life. The benefit of adopting non-dualism in a busy life is that it keeps the mentality constantly alert, mixing it with the experiences of actions, results and resolutions at all times. When one has to go through the state of absence of these experiences in peaceful times, then the person himself gets attracted towards Kundalini Yoga, because he is forced by the habit of awakened mentality. At that time, he is getting that awakened mentality from Kundalini only. If in the past he has lived with duality, then he is also used to lack of mentality, hence he is not able to get inspired in the right and interesting way towards Kundalini Yoga which keeps the mentality awake.

The monosyllabic that Premyogi Vajra had uttered for his own benefit when he was under the influence of his enlightenment, is as follows:-

There is no religion greater than humanity, no worship greater than work; No teacher is bigger than the problem, no monastery is bigger than the householder;

"There is no greater teacher/Guru than the problem", this above phrase is full of contradiction and mystery. It is absolutely true that without a Guru there is no knowledge, but it is also true that irreligious (inhuman) Gurus can be destructive as well, like religious extremists. Therefore, there is a need to walk with open eyes and not believe without thinking. It is also written that "There is no religion bigger than humanity". Guruseva is an integral part of humanity. There is one more thing. If someone does not have the desire to learn and know anything, then even the Guru cannot help him much. The desire to learn and know arises from problems only. Here humanity is balancing the problem, that is, the problem should not be so great that humanity itself gets endangered. Its second meaning also is that the small problems that come up while working, they themselves keep us moving forward by teaching us with proper guidance. There are many examples of this. This also does not mean that one should learn only from problems and not from experienced people, because the quality of learning from experienced people is also present in the above mentioned humanity itself. Another meaning of this is that the Guru cannot provide anything to someone who is just sitting. To achieve something, one has to struggle oneself, one has to face all the problems oneself, and one has to gain all the experiences oneself. Guru can only guide. It also means that a particular rule, religion, sect or any other relative process may not be equally beneficial for all people. Therefore, despite living within the bounded rules, one should keep wrestling in the world with Advaita here and there as per the problem. This is similar to the way domestic animals are not left completely free and are grazed in a limited area only, under supervision. If the rules passed down from family tradition are completely abandoned, then a situation of "not at home nor at no home" may also arise. Anyway, the problem itself tells which work, when and how to do it. If the pain is in the leg, what is the benefit of taking medicine for the head? "No worship is greater than work" and "No monastery is greater than a householder", both these phrases are the basic principles of Karmayoga and Tantra. The intelligent Premyogi Vajra understood all these things completely, that is why he has proved them and shown them in the presented book. "There is no worship greater than work, no religion greater than humanity", the mixed meaning of these two phrases is that no worship can be greater than work filled with humanity. This does not at all mean that worship and religion are small things; rather, it means that if a person pretends to worship or adopt religion while committing acts of inhumanity, then his worship or religion is not greater than the humanity of the humanist. In reality, God is not visible; rather, it is visible only in the form of its humane, nondual and non-attachment nature. Therefore, through this type of natural behaviour (human action), God is automatically worshiped and indirectly, attention to him also remains constant. Such behaviour develops very quickly in a person. In fact, Kama or Karma is a synonym for good work/good deeds. Bad work is called misdeed. Therefore, like a subtle subtle bodily being or dehapurush or body-man of Shavid, Doing work considering it as worship is the best devotion.

The religion of humanity is the real religion. Other man-made religions are only its cooperative parts. If they disregard it, then perhaps they will be considered worse than Adharma. Humanity means making efforts for the benefit of humanity at every time and in every situation. Just look at the body-men. They work continuously and tirelessly to make life possible for all of us. They have neither adopted any religion, nor read any religious book. But it is their natural instinct or tendency that they strive in every way for the welfare and development of humanity, with non-duality and non-attachment. Has that air studied any religion, which we breathe to live? No. But its natural tendency is to keep giving us life. Similarly; has the great Sun, Water, Fire and Mother Earth ever received a degree from any religious university? No. The natural tendency of all of them is to keep working with nonduality, in the interest of life. In this way, it is proved that religion naturally exists in nature, everywhere and at all times. Man has only copied that religion, to a greater or lesser extent.

Nowadays, there seems to be a situation of confusion over Ida-Pingala also. It's a simple thing. Sensations throughout the body are collected through the afferent nerve channel, and sent to the brain via the spinal cord. This nerve also expresses emotions and resolutions in the brain. There is more joy and light in it, due to which it falsely seems that another glimpse of enlightenment is about to come. Therefore, this nadi generates attraction and attachment. For this reason, Kundalini's natural desire is to remain in this nadi. Premyogi Vajra had also become enamoured with it in the same way, and had allowed his Kundalini to remain trapped in it. When he lagged far behind others physically, he took the shelter of Shavid and gave up his attachment to Ida and also allowed Kundalini to flow through the Pingala Nadi. Pingala Nadi (efferent nerve channel) passes through the spinal cord, emerges from the brain and spreads throughout the body, and issues orders to the entire body to perform actions. It is more practical and less experiential. Then, through Pingala, his Kundalini started spreading to all the karmendriyas or work-senses and the world. In this way his Kundalini started getting expressed equally and balanced everywhere. Then the Kundalini meditation of Premyogi Vajra started focusing equally on the sensations/emotions and behaviour/actions and he became samadhistha in a balanced manner. All that happened psychologically, the physiological aspect is only for understanding and explanation.

Nowadays, the trend of calling mental experiences like Kundalini as energy seems to be increasing, especially among the so-called modern class. Due to this, the importance of Kundalini and other spiritual experiences appears to be somewhat dwarfed. Energy is inanimate (non-living), whereas Kundalini or Shakti is animate (living). Ancient, meaningful and famous names should not be changed; No matter what caste, religion or sect it is associated with, because there is a divine inspirational power hidden in it. Calling conscious or living Kundalini as energy is as incomplete a description as calling the famous scientist Einstein e=mc square. The awakened Kundalini has all the qualities of consciousness, and is the best after Parabrahma or formless supreme; While energy can be inert, it can also have many types and levels; Due to this, spiritual progress can be slowed down, even stopped, and it can even show adverse effects etc. There is a lot of power in a name. From time immemorial, descendants of countless sages and yogis have been spreading the word Kundalini with their knowledge. They were universal, and were not bound by any caste, religion, race, region or tradition. Therefore they belong to everyone, and no one should hesitate in taking shelter of them. Experiencing strange sensations in different parts of the body, such as different lights, sounds, pricks and paralysis types etc.; it appears to be caused by improper focus on fixed or changing mental energy. This also happens when long-stored mental energy is suddenly released in an arbitrary and unprofitable manner, without proper guidance. There does not seem to be any possibility of any spiritual benefit or enlightenment from these. These and other strange symptoms that arise in a person probably arise due to resisting the Kundalini. The only way to avoid these side effects seems to be to convert the physical body of the Guru, Dev, Tantric consort etc. into Kundalini and concentrate on that mental picture. Kundalini is a life force. It is the guru, lover-consort, parents, relatives, wealth, gods etc. everything. It is the messenger of God. It is a miniature form of God that can be absorbed in the mind. It is the incarnation of God. It leads us to God. She is our protector. She is our guide. She benefits and develops us in every way, in return for which she only asks for a permanent residence in our own mind, nothing else. She is a unique form of love. She is our beloved. It nourishes the vital air and vitality, thereby keeping the body and mind healthy. She remains with us even when everything else leaves us. When the Yogi has been meditating regularly on Kundalini for about one and a half to two years, then he himself gets attracted towards God and starts immersing himself in His devotion, because God has a higher state than Kundalini. It is the natural instinct of the living being that it automatically keeps moving towards higher and higher states. If the same thought or picture keeps recurring in someone's mind for a long time, so that is the main symptom of his Kundalini awakening in the past. Same thing happened with Premyogi Vajra also. The pictures of Kundalini may change according to the state and environment, but the practice of continuous contemplation remains the same.

Around the completion of Shavid, Premyogi Vajra also had a momentary experience of Samadhi due to the additional force of Kundalini Yoga. The mental picture of the physical body strengthened by Kundalini Yoga had immediately matured in his mind. Premyogi Vajra's entire brain was filled with that Kundalini, and it was feeling heavy. The consciousness of ego, the world, and the body had ended, although the eyes were open and focused. The mental physical body was equally present everywhere, inside and outside. It seemed as if ordinary things were not separate from him, but were inside him. There was a feeling of immense joy, unity, peace and stress-freeness. Rationality had been destroyed, and only experience remained. Due to concern about his health and feeling ashamed of the people around; at the same time, Premyogi Vajra got scared of lack of awareness of self or ego. Due to this fear, he forcefully brought down Kundalini. According to Yoga Shastras, in such a state one should surrender oneself to Kundalini and should not try anything. The samadhi state lasted for about 5-10 seconds.

Premyogi Vajra describes his samadhi in his own words as follows, "I have been practicing Advaita (mainly Shavid, i.e. body science philosophy, coming through Sanatana Dharma fellowship) for 18 years, with a worldly approach full of practicality and hard work; irregular and incomplete (without focused concentration) yoga practice for about 10-11 years (with both these methods, my mental Kundalini remained alive in the base form/ Mooladhar); For the past one year, I was practicing Kundalini Yoga in a quiet and stress-free place, far away from my home, regularly and dedicatedly, by meditating on the Kundalini in the form of a mental picture of a very familiar old spiritual man (Guru, (This made my Kundalini mature, ; And since the last one month, by combining Tantricyoga/ Pratyakshayaunasansargayoga/direct sexual yoga (regularly/almost daily) with the above sadhna, I was making my Kundalini extremely mature/ upward moving/awakening oriented. After a long journey, I had returned home with my family in my new and personal vehicle. Then one day I was sitting on a chair at a function. Due to the calming effect of Kundalini Yoga-Sadhana, my beard had also grown to medium size, and about 30 percent of its hair appeared to be white. I was heartily welcomed at that function. There I was feeling special love and respect for me all around. It seemed as if my childhood memories associated with ceremonial people had become fresh. I was feeling open, safe, calm, stress free, mindful, non-dual and with the mental Kundalini picture. People related to my Kundalini were present there, and the environment was also related to my Kundalini. That house, built on a steep hill, seemed stuck to it. There was a lot of hustle and bustle there. Ceremonial music (of the modern kind) was also being played at a moderate level. It seemed as if the happy faces of familiar people were flying here and there, and coming up and down the stairs. I was in the balcony of the middle floor. In a room a group of women were busy dancing and singing. Sometimes one by one, sometimes in groups of two and in very rare cases in groups of three, the women would get up one by one, come into the middle of the circle of 20-25 women singing and display their dancing skills. The road in front of me, built straight on a green and vibrant hill and at almost the same height from the mountain peak, that was the height of that house, and from there the noise of the means of transport could be heard at a moderate level. The redness of the face of the sun on that front hill was increasing, as if it was eagerly waiting for the completion of its duty. I am meeting after a long time, an old and recently retired soldier, physically related to my mental Kundalini picture and having the same good nature as him, like full of qualities like hard work, my knowledgeable brother along with a friend, cheerful and bright. As soon as he started asking about my well-being with familiarity, I got deeply lost in the thought of my Kundalini and it got stimulated and suddenly took over my entire mind. My head became heavy and I started feeling pressure. That pressure in the brain was of a special form, because even ordinary pressure suppresses consciousness, but that pressure was provoking consciousness. It seemed as if the river of consciousness inside my brain was rotating with full speed in the form of a whirlpool and was making every particle of my brain vibrate, which my brain was unable to bear. It was happening. That fierce whirlpool of consciousness seemed to be creating an explosive pressure outwards in my brain. It seemed to me that my Kundalini was driving that consciousness whirl, because I was experiencing it everywhere. That kind of light, stormy, serious and similar sound was being experienced, the kind of sound produced by a swarm of bees flying together. In reality it was not even a sound, but something similar to it, filled with silence, filled with a strange kind of pressure or constriction of the brain, an experience of immense self-consciousness. The same pressure as is felt in the brain while doing Shirshasana or Sarvangasana; Although that experience was much more blissful matching somewhat a sexual bliss, with the silence mentioned above, it was conscious, light, Kundalini-filled and even say supremely type blissful. If an electric transformer experiences a secret rustling movement going on within it, filled with both silence and sound together (though not sound, but like sound), then it should consider it to be a state similar to Kundalini awakening. That was not even enlightenment, but an experience of a lower level than that. It was a feeling like the uniform and long drawn out sound of the middle syllable of Om, "O————————". It is possible that the secret of Om is also hidden in Kundalini awakening. Visual experiences also seem to be like a swarm of bees, desperate to burst the brain and get out. With a powerful flutter, as if the experience was trying to fly upward. There was a state of extreme joy. That pleasure was greater than hundreds of sexual intercourses together. The simple meaning is that the senses cannot generate that much pleasure. Kundalini was completely illuminated and was competing the sun. It seemed more clear, alive and real than the physical objects of reality. Eyes were open and seriously looking at the sights. Wherever the vision was going, Kundalini was visible there. It seemed as if everything was colored in the colors of Kundalini. All experiences seemed identical, unchanged or non-dual and complete. My ego was completely destroyed. I was getting worried about my health. I had no sense of my personality. The 2-3 people sitting on the chair next to me, that friend/acquaintance and some people passing by also started looking at me with surprise, doubt and possibly a little worry, due to which I started feeling a little hesitant. I bowed my head a little and repeatedly rubbed the upper border of my forehead with the tips of my right hand and squeezed my eyes and tried to come back to my personality. After some efforts the Kundalini came back down. I realized my mistake and tried to raise the Kundalini back up, but I could not succeed, although I felt very happy, refreshed, stress-free and full of non-attachment/duality. At the time of that experience of Kundalini awakening, I was feeling warmth and redness on my face. I had such an experience even during indirect Tantra, when the picture of the first goddess used to become clear and intense in my mind, though at a moderate level compared to this Kundalini awakening. This time, the picture was not of Devi Rani, but of that Puranapathi old spiritual man (who has been described in the introduction/dedication part of the book), the picture was experienced most clearly and intensely, though only for 10 seconds. The picture of the first goddess always remained in the mind; sometimes in mild level, sometimes in moderate level and sometimes in severe level. Although this time the picture of Kundalini was expressed at the highest level. The mental picture (Kundalini) of the old spiritual man also remained almost always (though for a less time than that of the goddess), but it was mostly expressed at a mild level; relatively little at moderate or severe levels. It seems that my physical and sex-oriented environment was responsible for such differences. Had there been a spiritual environment, perhaps the opposite would have happened, that is, the mental picture of an old spiritual man would have been more powerful than that of the goddess. The picture of the goddess never expressed itself beyond the level of its physical form, but in this Kundalini awakening, the picture of the old spiritual man expressed itself even beyond the level of its physical form. That experience had loosened the noose of womanhood in my mind, because the formation of the most vivid mental picture, even without sexual arousal, was no less than a surprise. I never experienced complete samadhi (awakened Kundalini) with the mental picture of the first Devi Rani (active Kundalini), that is, that Kundalini remained active continuously, but could never be awakened. However, with time, the Second Goddess Queen, by providing direct/ complete Tantra Yoga/Leftist Tantra help, raised and awakened the Kundalini in the form of the mental picture of that old spiritual man in my body. Probably, this Kundalini awakening/Samadhi is said to be the joining/ uniting of Kundalini with Parabrahma/Soul in Sahasrara Chakra/brain.

It may be possible that people feel that Premyogi Vajra is going crazy or ill. This also leads to the conclusion that most of the so-called mad people are Kundalini-yogis. In reality, their Kundalini has been awakened, hence they keep searching and seeing their Kundalini in everything, and sometimes even start talking to it. In fact, at the time of Kundalini awakening, Premyogi Vajra's mental eye was opened. This is also called the third eye or sixth sense. This mental eye is much more subtle, joyful, peaceful, luminous and insightful than the physical eyes. Near Kundalini awakening, a surge-like pressure of Kundalini, in a subtle and latent form, is felt in the body and mind, which keeps inspiring for Kundalini awakening. That surge calms down only after Kundalini awakening. Then to awaken the Kundalini again, that energy has to be accumulated, which takes more or less time, depending on the effort towards sadhana. When Kundalini Yoga is accomplished, then there is a divine state of mind filled with peace, stresslessness, non-duality and bliss. Additionally, firmness is present in the sexual restraint of sex yoga. Immediately after yoga practice, appetite increases suddenly, and if you overeat, it also decreases during the next meal. Then it increases again during the next meal, and the cycle continues like this. Probably this happens only to keep the body weight balanced. Kundalini is very intelligent, and for its maximum expression, it considers appropriate and balanced weight to be the best. Nevertheless, it is beneficial to eat under control at that time, otherwise there is a possibility of indigestion, laziness and laxity. While eating dry food (chapati, biscuits etc.), even if we eat as per our stomach, after some time the stomach starts feeling heavy, because dry foods swell by absorbing water. The way to avoid this seems to be to drink some water while eating, which reduces the amount of food required to fill the stomach. This also improves digestion, although excess water may cause some problems.

If the mind is stressed, remembering something or continuously focusing on the same picture, then a pressure/heaviness is felt on the mind or head. So just think, when that picture becomes as clear as it is alive and real, then how much and what kind of pressure would be felt. Premyogi Vajra also felt the same pressure. Kundalini awakening mostly happens suddenly at a time when there seems to be no possibility of its awakening, and the person is living in a mindful, happy and social environment. Same thing happened with Premyogi Vajra that is why he could not prepare to keep the Kundalini in Sahasrara for a long time. This also means that we should never sit expecting Kundalini awakening. When awakening has to happen, it can happen on its own and at any time under favourable circumstances. If there were expectations, it might have played blindly. Nevertheless, in that period of time, when there is silence in the mind along with the above mentioned divine symptoms and there is also increased heaviness and pressure, the possibility of Kundalini awakening is more in that period. When there is already a pressure of Sadhana in the brain and along with it, the pressure of Kundalini awakening is also suddenly added to it, then it is natural that it is a little difficult to bear that experience, although perhaps with practice and fearlessness, it will become better in time. It becomes bearable. Premyogi Vajra probably brought down the Kundalini because he was so scared in his subconscious mind of the terrible mental conditions arising from his earlier momentary self-realisation and the physical disturbances arising from them. As soon as he experienced, he unconsciously put that experience down. In principle, one should not be afraid of Kundalini, one should love it, allow it to appear as per one's wish, should not create obstacles in its desired activities and should remain dedicated to it. Premyogi Vajra had not heard, read and understood well that the awakened Kundalini should not be brought down. It is also a matter of great surprise that we can never tell with complete accuracy when Kundalini awakening will happen, we can only express the possibility. That is why one should not be in a hurry and should not be restless for Kundalini awakening. One should continue to meditate as comfortable as possible. The phenomenon of Kundalini awakening seems simple, but still it cannot be completely controlled.

Premyogi Vajra did not feel his Kundalini crawling upwards like a serpent. Nor did he feel the Kundalini penetrating the chakras. He only felt as if he was lost in the thought of Kundalini. In reality, the mental picture of a man being remembered is called Kundalini. When that memory takes an extreme form and crosses a certain limit, then the same Kundalini becomes awakened Kundalini, as experienced by Premyogi Vajra in the above description. From the above description, it appears that many things related to Kundalini may have been created to attract the illusionary, philosophical and common people towards Kundalini Yoga, but on the contrary, these things can sometimes confuse and discourage the curious people. It may also happen that a very high level Kundalini Yogi experiences these miraculous events, but common seekers do not seem to get any benefit from them, because they only want Kundalini awakening, no matter in any human way. Let it happen. According to the author, when Kundalini Yoga is practiced regularly for about one and a half years, then along with the contraction of Vajra, many times the Kundalini located above it is also felt to be moving, moving up, and starts getting expressed in the brain. This happens especially when the Tantric consort is also present. Even while practicing yoga, Premyogi Vajra could never clearly see the Kundalini on its way up from Muladhara to the brain (Ajna Chakra). After Yogabandh was applied, he felt it disappearing in the perineum and appearing in the brain. As another proof of this, on page 306 of Joseph Campbell's book (a mythical image), Sri

Ramakrishna Paramhansa says that I have to find my Kundalini sometimes crawling like an insect or a snake and sometimes jumping straight up like a monkey. The brain itself is called Ajna Chakra. Premyogi Vajra did not experience any specific place of Ajna Chakra, like it has been said to be in the middle of the eyebrows or on its straight edge, right at the back of the head, etc. He also paid little attention to the Kundalini between the eyebrows. He meditated only in the mind, call it Agya Chakra or something else. The brain chakra appears to be only one. The only difference is the height in different chakras of the brain. Sahasrara Chakra is located at the highest place in the brain. In fact, in the Sahasrar Chakra, Kundalini is considered to be established only at the time of awakening (the above 10 seconds of Samadhi). Although he did not feel his Kundalini rising above the Muladhara (root chakra), he felt it in his brain with a strong and silent pressure denoting its rising. This means that probably with the heavy help of sex yoga; Kundalini was awakened very quickly at that time, when even his lower chakras were not completely unblocked, although with the help of great sexual power, Kundalini jumped and reached Sahasrara straight. Probably it happened in the same way as lightning from thundering clouds, breaking even the barrier of the atmosphere, jumps and enters the earth. Similarly, Kundalini can be any strange or unfamiliar object or inanimate energy (light, sound, etc., which appears suddenly); or when it is ignited by continuous sadhana, it is only a special mental picture (of Guru, Ishtadev etc.), which can awaken in Sahasrara at any time. It is possible that the mental picture of a particular light or sound etc. may also become awakened, but that awakening is also possible only through regular and prolonged meditation, not suddenly or like a flower falling from the sky. People may call their forgotten past act as sudden. In fact, the simplest and most practical solution is to meditate on Kundalini in the form of a familiar, mindful and auspicious human figure, as Premyogi Vajra did.

In that samadhi, Premyogi Vajra experienced everything inside his mind. The sights outside, sounds outside, other feelings outside, thoughts inside, etc. are all experiences; everything was experienced equally in the mind. It was natural to experience this way, because the mental Kundalini experience was the most intense and bright, hence how could other lower level experiences appear to be external, because it is a common experiential belief that external experiences are intense, while mental experiences are weak. That is why when the experience of pure mental Kundalini was more intense than all the external experiences, then all the external experiences themselves became pure mental (inner) experiences. Because all experiences existed in the brain, all experiences appeared to be the same, because how could experiences located in the same brain (together, consisting of the same types of sensations) with same intensity appear to be different from each other.

When Kundalini gets completely ignited inside the brain in the form of complete blissful samadhi, even once and even for a moment, then it probably starts attracting the seeker towards itself, and gradually takes him to enlightenment. All mental pictures together cannot be ignited more than their physical forms, that is why only one picture is taken as a sample, and it is strengthened through repeated practice to reach the state of Samadhi. Probably the same process continues even after Kundalini awakening, which happened with Premyogi Vajra through the meditation of Pratham Devirani in the past. That is the state of Samprajnata Samadhi. Kundalini is almost always present in the mind due to which the experienced world gets connected with it. Then when the age of mental Kundalini is completed, it starts to dissolve, along with which the world connected to it also starts to dissolve. When Kundalini becomes void, the world also becomes void, and a blissful emptiness prevails in the mind of the Yogi. In reality it is a virtual emptiness, not a real one, because the experienced world remains the same as before, only the attachment towards it becomes void. That is the state of asamprajnata samadhi. Momentary enlightenment can occur at any time in the midst of that. Probably the same thing happened with Yogi Sri Ramakrishna Paramahansa. His meditation was so strong that Kali Mata was clearly visible to him everywhere and all the time. When his Guru saw that he was not able to go beyond that state of Samprajnata Samadhi, he asked him to destroy Kali Mata. As soon as the mental picture of Kali Mata was destroyed, he became situated in Asamprajnata Samadhi, due to which he attained enlightenment.

Probably the Kundalini of Premyogi Vajra had reached Sahasrara, and he could not keep it there for the time required for enlightenment (probably around a minute on average). This theory is that Kundalini suddenly reaches Sahasrara at that time, when the Kundalini seeker gets a favourable environment for Kundalini. For example, if a Kundalini seeker has been meditating on the Kundalini in the form of Mahadev for a long time and in the midst of his meditation, he ever goes on a pilgrimage to the holy Kailash, then the possibility of his Kundalini reaching Sahasrara becomes extremely strong. Similarly, if a person is meditating intensely on the Kundalini of his late grandfather (Guru) in solitude with the help of sex yoga, then if after a long time he wants to meet his relatives or guru brothers. If someone has a loving relationship with his Guru, then during his interaction with them, his Kundalini suddenly gets immense strength, due to which it becomes alive and awakens. In fact, the relationship with them is also established through the same grandfather as being a common ancestor of, and that reconciliation too. Therefore, at that time, remembering the grandfather becomes an obligation on both sides. If those acquaintances start showing heartfelt love, then Kundalini will automatically receive that power of love, because it is only with her shelter and cooperation that we have relationships with acquaintances. In such a situation the possibility of Kundalini awakening increases immensely. Anyway, the mental picture of that grandfather already had become very strong due to daily yoga practice. In such a situation, his strong memory on the occasion of that meeting gives a lot of mental strength to that picture, and it comes alive in the form of Kundalini awakening. This is just an example. Similarly, if there is a strong possibility of strong and all-round remembrance of a mental picture anywhere, then that picture comes alive in the form of Kundalini awakening. Such a possibility increases manifold if Advaita has been studied and applied in life through Shavid etc. for years. Probably, with regular Kundalini Yoga practice for a long time, no such expectation is required and Kundalini awakening occurs directly through Yoga practice. Such a possibility can also be created by excessive and continuous fear, as was created in Kansa by the fear of Krishna. Such a possibility can also be created through extreme love, as was created in Meera who was crazy about Krishna. Such a possibility can also be created due to extreme hatred, as was created in Shishupal who was mad with hatred for Krishna. The Kundalini in the form of the mental picture of Krishna had become active or awakened in the minds of all of them.

This misconception is also prevalent that enlightenment takes place only in the mountains. If it were so then all the hill people would be enlightened. In fact, most of the enlightened hill people who are described have moved from the plains to the mountains in search of peace. Premyogi Vajra also had momentary enlightenment only when he entered into a period of deep friendship with the students/people who had come from the plains, especially Rajasthan and Punjab, and had been living in the mountains since ancient times. Therefore, the mixture of mountains and plains definitely has some contribution in enlightenment. Anyway, in the open plain situated at the end of the mountain, one experiences a surprising peace of enlightenment, as is also visible on the borders of hilly regions and plain regions (for example in Rishikesh-Haridwar). In fact, most of the people living in the mountains are very close to enlightenment, because by nature they are hardworking, Tantric, humble and dualist. They only need a little additional spiritual power to cross the limits of the physical dimension, but they are not able to make real and sufficient efforts. Even guidance related to spiritual practice is not easily accessible to them. Due to the difficult life of the people in the mountains, they are not able to pay proper attention to sadhana. It is because of the pleasant and harmonious life of the mountains and the fresh climate that they come so close to enlightenment. They are also more humble and happy. The main reason for all these divine qualities is that they are staunch devotees of the local deities, who appear to Premyogi Vajra to be as almighty as the body-man or dehpurush of Shavid.

Premyogi Vajra describes his Samadhikaraka Kundalini Yoga in his own words as follows, "I used to practice Kundalini Yoga twice a day, for at least one and a half hour in the morning and one hour in the evening, about the same time every day. And at fixed time. First of all, I used to do yoga asanas while meditating on Kundalini on different chakras as per the asanas. Food etc. was not eaten till at least four hours before, and drinks like water etc. were not drunk till one hour before. It provided protection from possible stomach diseases (gastric oesophageal acid reflux, hiatal hernia, piles/ haemorrhoids etc.). Yoga also reduces the size of the abdomen to some extent. Very little stool begins to be produced, because most of the food eaten is digested by the power of prana and absorbed by the body. I used to do the asanas which put less pressure on the stomach in the evening and the asanas which put more pressure on the stomach in the morning. Then I used to sit in Siddhasana, and while meditating on Kundalini on Muladhar, I used to do Kapalbhati and Anulom-Vilom Pranayam. After that I used to do microcosmic orbit, which is a simple counterpart of Kundalini rotation. In this, the breath was held after inhaling and exhaling, while meditating on Kundalini on each chakra. I used to hold my breath as easily as possible; initially, I used to do it by inhaling and exhaling just like in a normal situation. In the first rotation process, I used to inhale through the left nostril and exhale through the right nostril. At the beginning of the process, the Kundalini was taken up from Muladhara to the brain with the help of Bandhas. In the initial stage of Kundalini Yoga, it seemed as if by applying Yogikbandha, the pressure of the unknown and internal vital air (not gross air) would rise upwards, and reach the brain with a sensation like a micro-explosion, with which the Kundalini was also stuck. Then I used to rotate the Kundalini clockwise in the brain (like a farmer ploughing). The farmer used to be meditated while using the plough, leveller etc., scraping the walls of the brain, then ploughing in circular circles, going inwards. It felt like a real scratching, with a pressure on the brain. Many times I was afraid that some deformity might occur in the brain, because there is a lot of power in meditation, but nothing like this happened. Such scratching also increased the intensity of meditation and the brain felt refreshed. I could feel the sound of the leveller hitting the outer and rocky shores around my brain, like a thump. This also refreshed the mind. Perhaps these may have also helped in Kundalini awakening, because due to this, I had become accustomed to bear the situation of pressure and sensation in the brain at the time of Kundalini awakening. This also had the benefit that every part of my brain became active, which is necessary for Kundalini awakening. Even at the time of Kundalini awakening, my entire brain was filled to the brim with Kundalini. If any part of the brain remains dormant or lethargic, then Kundalini awakening cannot possibly occur. Then I would touch the tongue with the soft palate, and I kept touching it until kundalini reached the Swadhishthana Chakra. Kundalini descends from the brain through the path of the tongue and settles on the designated chakra. Then, through Moolabandha, it remains fixed on the same chakra with the necessary upward pressure. First, I used to lower the Kundalini till the Vishuddhi

Chakra (at the base of the neck, towards the front), as if a farmer has come down after ploughing the field and is resting. Then the Kundalini-Kisan would descend till the heart chakra (between the two breasts, the real home of the farmer). After taking rest, Kundalini-Farmer would reach the Nabhi-Chakra field with his plough and oxen. Then the circular navel area was ploughed anti clockwise. There too, I used to meditate on the farmer while ploughing the entire abdominal area from outside to inside. Then he would descend to Svadhisthana Chakra (near the base of the Vajra) to rest. After that, he would remain calm at his most native place i.e. Muladhara Chakra (right in the middle of the perineum, i.e. the midline going from the anus to the testicles), or he would be working in a light manner. Kundalini appeared most clearly there, and the special thing is that even during busy and worldly work, Kundalini could be meditated there easily. While inhaling, I used to meditate in such a way that the Kundalini was getting strengthened by drinking the vital air. After Samadhi/Kundalini awakening, I had also learned to merge Prana and Apana together, in which I used to meditate on taking the breath to Kundalini, and after applying Moolabandha, Apana (Prana of lower parts of the body) would rise up and Prana (vital air of upper body) would fall down over Kundalini. Used to meditate on both getting mixed up. Due to this, the Kundalini simultaneously received the power of Prana from above and Apana from below, and it got ignited doubly. To apply Moolabandha, the muscles of the perineum were contracted in such a way that upward pressure was created and the anus was also constricted upward. From time to time, depending on the situation, I also took the help of Uddiyana Bandha. In this, while exhaling and inhaling a little, he used to contract his stomach inwards and lift it upwards. Due to this, the Kundalini was moving upwards

, especially from Muladhar directly to Ajna Chakra (Brain Chakra). Every time after inhaling and exhaling, Jalandhar bandh was applied, so that the prana is locked and could not escape upward or away from the Kundalini and could not create any other air disorders. That bandha was applied by bending the neck and head down and bringing the chin close to the chest. This entire process was then completed by inhaling through the right nostril and exhaling through the left. In this, the Kundalini in the brain and navel chakras was rotated in the opposite direction from the first process. In the third rotation process, breath was taken and exhaled from both the nostrils. In that, the meditation of Kundalini in the brain and navel chakras was done again in the direction of the first process (that time by using the farmer-Kundalini leveller). When I completed one year of practicing in this type manner or whatever style suiting with ease (without breaking the practice even once), Kundalini Yoga was combined with Tantric sexual intercourse to give enlightening and empowering power to Kundalini.

If in the initial period it seems difficult to meditate on Kundalini on some chakras (especially the cervical, svadhisthana and heart chakra etc.), then meditation can be done by touching them. As mentioned above, the cervical chakra is like a depression just below the high part of the throat, where it is supposed to be flat. There is a sensational experience there. It is approximately 6 fingers above the lower end of the triangular pit that connects the chest and throat. The neck can also be bent slightly backwards, which creates a little pressure on the cervical chakra, which stimulates the Kundalini a bit. Similarly, the heart chakra is located in between or slightly above both the breasts. Swadhisthana Chakra is located slightly (about three fingers) above the root of the genital organ, above the bone, where it is pressed and forms a depression, and a sexual sensation is experienced. The Swadhisthana Chakra of the spine is located about 5-6 fingers above the lower end of the spine, where when pressed, a depression is formed, and an intense sensation is experienced. In reality, everything becomes known through practice, because the clearest picture of Kundalini itself is formed at a special and sensitive place.

It becomes clear from the above description that once the basic Kundalini Yoga is perfected, tantric sexual intercourse becomes very easy, positive and intensely beneficial. There is no need to be confused regarding the chakras. These are symbolic. Meditation can be done anywhere in the body, because the body-men means dehpurushas are present everywhere, both inside the body and outside the body (as we have proved in the sharirvigyan darshan). Meditation feels better where one feels stiffness/ sensation due to bending etc., because there the body is getting swelled with adequate blood supply. Because the maximum stiffness is felt on the chakras and spine while doing yoga, that is why Kundalini meditation is said to be easy there. Accordingly, the chakras continue in the depth of the entire body (from the front part of the body to the back part, i.e. the spine). However, if meditation is done daily on a specific area/chakra, then meditation is more beneficial, in the same way, eating food at a specific place and time is beneficial for the stomach. With regular practice, by applying Moolabandha and Uddeyaan Bandha, the Kundalini is gradually felt rising on its own through the front channel. That Uddiyanabandha is the best which is felt by itself. In this, after some time of applying Moolabandha, when the breath feels like a suffocation, or a short breath is taken from the chest, then the stomach itself goes inwards a little, and along with it, the middle of the body including the abdomen tuck up to the shoulders, means the part shrinks slightly upwards. This increases the flow of prana towards the brain. That prana energizes the Kundalini in the brain. By the way, it is good to apply Moolabandha along with Uddiyanabandha, otherwise by applying only Moolabandha, it keeps falling loose. When the stomach moves upwards due to Laghu Uddiyanabandha, it becomes easier to apply upward pressure to apply Moolabandha. Through Yogabandhas, the Prana rises upwards and strengthens the same mental picture i.e. Kundalini, keeping in mind the Yogabandhas. This means that Yogabandha also works on the principle of fixed targeting. In Siddhasana, there is a pressure on the Muladhar Chakra from the heel of the foot, due to which the Kundalini also gets some force to rise up. Probably, many excellent seekers also feel the Kundalini rising up through the spine. It should be allowed to remain in its natural place and should not be pushed upwards or downwards with too much force. Then it keeps rising on its own with the power of bandhas. Its reaching the brain does not mean its final round. It keeps going up and down for a long time, and gradually matures in the brain. When it becomes completely mature, it transforms into the above mentioned form of Purnasamadhi (Kundalini awakening), that is, it enters Sahasrara. Although some level of samadhi is always experienced, the door to liberation is only complete samadhi. While practicing, one starts to experience which Bandha and breath is appropriate, because the orientation of Kundalini towards light or expression is itself guiding the astute seeker. Natural samadhi/sexual samadhi is achieved itself for day and night without any effort. Just as Premyogi Vajra used to feel during adolescence, at the time of momentary self-realization. Artificial Samadhi occurs only in the morning or evening, in the middle of the practice of Kundalini Yoga, although Purna Samadhi (Kundalini awakening) can occur at any time. In fact, artificial samadhi should not be applied forcefully and during the day, because it can have adverse effects on the rational actions of the dehapurusha. With long-term practice, even artificial samadhi becomes so strong that it continues day and night just like natural samadhi. Natural Samadhi mostly occurs due to very intense and spontaneously arising sexual attraction, as happened with Premyogi Vajra. The practice of Kundalini diverts the seeker from useless materialism and takes him towards mentality/spirituality, because while experiencing the shining Kundalini first in his body, then in his mind and brain and finally in his soul, the seeker comes to know that the reality and Importance lies within the mind and soul, not in the outside world. When Samadhi becomes a habit, then without it the world begins to seem meaningless and harmful. Therefore, even before one samadhi is completely over, the seeker takes refuge in another samadhi. Samadhi is the same, only its mental picture changes. New Samadhi can be achieved naturally, through the principle of transference, and can also be achieved afresh through spiritual practice. In those men who are bright, intelligent and concentrated during childhood, the effect of samadhi of their previous birth is visible. Samadhi works as a mental cover, which protects the mind from dual worldly sufferings. Even after attaining enlightenment, a man automatically attains the protection of Samadhi. In fact, that shelter is already available, because enlightenment is achieved only through Samadhi. Later, even while doing Yogasana, Premyogi vajra had learned the art of connecting prana and apana by inhaling and holding the breath and simultaneously applying moolabandha. He started meditating on Kundalini inside the idol of worship, inside the Sun while offering water and inside Sanskrit verses while reading the Puranas. In fact, worship, self-study etc. provide full results only if Kundalini is meditated within them. The idols of Gods are mainly made from golden colored and shiny metals, such as gold, copper etc. This is done because in its state of activation and awakening, Kundalini appears golden and shining. Therefore, Kundalini should be seen and meditated on the shining surface of those idols. At the time of puja, we smell incense/flowers etc., see lights etc., eat bhog etc., hear bells etc. etc.; All those experiences rise up with the life force and strengthen the Kundalini. The meaning of

Prana here is the subtle Prana not the air, which rises above the Yogbandhas, and by raising the Kundalini also, keeps strengthening it in the brain. Direct attention is given to the chakras only, it automatically reaches the brain. Although one can meditate directly on the brain, but the Kundalini raised up from the sexual chakras is very powerful. Anyway, in practical life, it is difficult to concentrate directly in the brain.

After some practice, instead of meditating directly on the Chakra, meditating automatically through Prana is better, easier and more playful. While inhaling, one should meditate on the vital air entering the chakra. While exhaling, just as the Kundalini picture on the chakra begins to fade, the second, fuller breath reaches there, and the picture begins to shine again. This sequence continues like this. Movement of the abdomen on the navel chakra and svadhisthana chakra also helps in concentrating the prana. The movement of the chest on the heart chakra also provides some help. Prana can be concentrated on the Ajna Chakra (between the eyebrows) by slightly contracting the muscles of the forehead. By clenching the teeth a little and applying pressure on the Vishuddhi Chakra of the throat, prana can be concentrated there. Prana can be concentrated on the Mooladhara Chakra through momentary Moolabandha. Similarly, during Yogasana, it also helps in concentrating the Pranavayu on the spasm of the joints. Just as only a spark and air are sufficient to ignite a fire, in the same way Pranayama and Kundalini are required to ignite the fire of Yoga. Just as the same spark, when it comes in contact with air, becomes a raging flame of fire, so does Kundalini. Simply, once the meditation on the Kundalini Chakra starts and Pranayam keeps on infusing the vital air on it like a bellows, then it starts flaring up on its own, and becomes clearer, requiring more emphasis on the mind for deep meditation. The Kundalini Chakra gets strengthened by the vital air in the same way as the hearth of fire gets strengthened by the blowing of the wind. Just as the fire of the stove itself gets strengthened by the air, in the same way also the Kundalini of the Kundalini Chakra, because the body-man is present in every atom of the body, and the Kundalini, a personified form given to all the body-men, has the shape and form of a beloved human being. It is as per the theory of Shavid. Just as fire itself attracts air, so does Kundalini. Wherever there is Kundalini, the life or vital air itself gets drawn there. Similarly, wherever Prana is meditated, Kundalini manifests itself. In this way, Kundalini, Prana and meditation keep reinforcing each other.

If there is light breathing, then it should be poured on the Vishuddhi Chakra and if sufficient time and peace is available, then by applying Moola Bandha and Uddiyana Bandha, one should also meditate on the lower prana and its ascent to it. A little longer breaths should be poured onto the heart chakra. Moderate breaths should be poured on the navel chakra. Meditation should be done on long and deep breaths, pouring them over Swadhisthana and Muladhara. In this way, because the chakras are filled with Pranavayu, they can be said to be making the Kundalini clear and dynamic there and also rotating it in a way like a wind mill, perhaps that is why these special meditation points are called Chakras. . When the Kundalini fire is ignited by the life force of the entire body, it starts rotating in a circular motion, as if a farmer is ploughing a circular field at high speed. Chakravasini Kundalini is a living human form (Guru, Ishtadev etc.), which is superimposed on the living body-part, chakra or body-man. Through Kundalini Yoga, she herself continues to inhale the breath poured on the chakra, and continues to become strong, like the body-man described in the Shavid. There is still confusion regarding the opening of the Kundalini Chakras. Perhaps the opening of a chakra means that the Kundalini picture on that chakra is very clear, bright, alive and joyful. This simply means that the Kundalini can rise up from there for awakening at any time, otherwise in the state of closure of the Chakra, it keeps revolving on the Chakra itself. Premyogi Vajra had also experienced his Kundalini in the same opened-chakra form for several days before Kundalini awakening, on Muladhar, Swadhisthana and Ajna (brain) chakras.

Many people mistake Kundalini activation for Kundalini awakening, almost the same as Premyogi Vajra had understood before Kundalini awakening. When Kundalini becomes active, it becomes visible in daily life, here and there in the body, especially in the brain. Even during the practice of Kundalini Yoga, it continues to reach the Sahasrara (brain) along with each chakra of the body as specified; although there it will not be called awakened but active. When awakened, one experiences the same tremendous experience as described by Premyogi Vajra. The awakened Kundalini appears to be complete and most alive or true in the brain. She appears to be more alive than the physical world outside (as Premyogi Vajra experienced in the above mentioned 10 second samadhi). Under normal circumstances, Kundalini awakening is possible only through sexual yoga, because Kundalini awakening requires immense mental strength, which can be achieved only through sexual yoga. If the seeker is not of practical type but is of Sanyasi type, then in that situation Kundalini can be awakened even by simple Kundalini Yoga, because in that state of great peace, immense mental power can be easily attained. While doing sadhana, when the most accessible picture gets settled in the mind, that is, Kundalini becomes active, then its light gradually starts increasing due to the power of sadhana. Then it is natural that the mind starts paying more and more attention to it, because the mind itself runs after joyful and luminous things. At last that Kundalini awakens. Then the mind becomes completely satisfied, and all taste goes away, just as a man stops eating food after his stomach is full. Then the mind keeps running towards it, even during worldly practical times, without any sadhana, until continuous samadhi is achieved. Although many quality-loving seekers keep meditating vigorously on that Kundalini with regular sadhana. Perhaps this is even a better thing.

It is easy to meditate on Kundalini in Pranavayu or breath, i.e. pure, fresh and somewhat cool air (like that of the mountains). Due to such wind the flame of Kundalini gets ignited and flares up. Even in the physical world of reality, such breezes fill the mind with sweet thoughts. For this reason, most of the yogis and seekers practice Kundalini meditation while traveling in pure, clean and secluded mountains or in an otherwise open environment. By applying Moolabandha, when the vital air of the entire body reaches the brain with a rustle, the Kundalini starts glowing there. Sufficient oxygen is available even while travelling. During both direct and indirect samadhi, Premyogi Vajra was provided with such calm, free, solitary, and full of travel, clean, pure, yoga-yukt and limited labour etc. situations, full of vital air. If there is life and air, everything is there. This is life, this is progress, this is Kundalini awakening, this is self-knowledge, and this is liberation.

Just as success is not achieved in the field of physical sciences without following the theoretical rules, similarly in psychological sciences like Kundalini Yoga too. Even God cannot ignore these theoretical rules, although He can create favourable conditions for following them. Many great hard workers achieve success even in adverse circumstances. This proves that just like in the material aspect, in the spiritual aspect also, God is the only supporting reason for success, the main reason is to work hard in the right way. Most of the people, out of ignorance, consider God to be the main reason for spiritual success. Therefore, to attain the favour of God, remaining non-dual like the subtle subtle bodily being and doing all the works considering it as service to God is the real worship of God.

Premyogi Vajra was in constant touch with Kundalini related social media (Brilliano kundalini forum, emergingsciencefoundation.org) for almost a whole year under this above mentioned Samadhi producing Yoga Sadhana, and kept talking/chatting a lot related to Kundalini Yoga. Along with this, Premyogi was also continuously taking help of physical books, e-books and Quora (question-answer type online forum) related to Kundalini and practical spirituality. He was most influenced by books related to Tantric and sexual yoga. From the very beginning, he continued to take inspiration from there and also kept inspiring other members. This means that social-media association can also work, especially if the curiosity and hard work is intense. In the above chatting, Premyogi Vajra proved that knowledge arises from the relationship with opposite time zones, because due to this, day and night, i.e. light and darkness, get mixed together, due to which a unique Advaita is created. .

Premyogi Vajra explains the other benefits of Kundalini Yoga in his own words, "My mental depression and boredom diminished while doing Kundalini Yoga. My appetite had improved dramatically, and I was no longer worried about my body weight. But even before I gained weight, my appetite used to become normal on its own. The unnecessary noise in the mind had stopped. The troubling old memories had faded. Earlier I used to feel lonely and cut off from society, but with the practice of yoga I felt that society was lonely and cut off from me. The minor diseases of my digestive system were almost eradicated. The pain in my body had ended. I felt in a good state of mind throughout the day. Mental disorders were calmed down. Anger had come under control. My mind started working." In this way, we can see that through Kundalini Yoga, the results of both physical exercise and spiritual yoga practice are obtained simultaneously. It also provides some benefit in piles, because by applying Moolabandha, the contraction and expansion of the anus continues continuously, due to which the blood circulation in the related area is not obstructed. Kundalini Yoga is best after morning walk, toilet and bath. The mental illness of feeling dirt everywhere can also be destroyed by regular Kundalini Yoga.

Pranayama works like rain. Just as rain water seeps into the entire ground, in the same way the vital air of Pranayam also seeps into the entire body. Just as the water that has seeped into the ground is collected through water dams and small and big canals and the plants are irrigated with it, in the same way, the prana that has seeped into the body is poured onto the Kundalini with the use of Yogic Bandhas. Due to which the Kundalini gets strengthened and awakens.

At some places, this belief is also prevalent that doing wrong work even once does not lead to Kundalini awakening or enlightenment, as can be read in the scriptures also. For example, at one place it is written that the number of drops of alcohol consumed is equal to the number of births required for salvation. Perhaps this kind of fear has been created only to motivate towards the right path, in reality this does not seem to be happening, because Premyogi Vajra had also committed many wrongful conducts before attaining enlightenment and Kundalini awakening. He had smoked 2-4 times in his childhood, before his momentary enlightenment. Even before Kundalini awakening, for some time he had consumed alcohol, smoked, eaten meat, engaged in indirect anti-social sexual behaviour, and even consumed intoxicants. This does not at all mean that such behaviour should be done to awaken the Kundalini, rather it means that if someone is surrounded by these behaviours, then there is no need to be discouraged, because he can also improve his Kundalini by improving himself intensely. Although in the above case, Premyogi Vajra may be an exception, because he had also achieved extreme closeness to his Guru, yet with firm practice all tasks become possible.

Most of the people want that all the evils should be completely eliminated from the society. This desire is against the good order of the body-country, because the small evils necessary for a healthy society are present there too. All people of the society should be allies of each other, not opponents; as it happens in the body-country means Dehdesh. Mutual fights have never benefited anyone and it will never happen. Well, self-defense is everyone's birth right. Now take Premyogi Vajra, he had received the power of momentary soul knowledge also from a Rajoguna and Tamoguna dominated society. Even since childhood, Premyogi Vajra was brought up in a mixed type of society. Every type of human being lived there in harmony with each other. At that time, spiritual and sexual romance was also prevalent around Premyogi Vajra. It seemed as if he had tantric qualities since childhood. By being close to women, especially virtuous women, he experienced a higher mentality or rather, a mentality arising from the experience of self-knowledge. He considered women to be worshiped like goddesses. However, at the same time, he also expected women to be loving, sweet-spoken, tolerant, humorous, happy and with other feminine qualities and also to strive for the all-round progress of their husbands. Because a man comes under the control of a woman through loving behaviour, it is necessary that the woman supports and teaches proper conduct and thoughts. Same thing happened with Premyogi Vajra, when in the signal without words, Pratham Devi Rani means first tantric consort or queen had strongly condemned drinking, intoxication etc. This kept him from intoxicating substances, which was also an additional favourable reason in his momentary enlightenment. It is a matter of research whether tantric qualities had arisen in him due to the tantric influence of that area, or whether that area was filled with sexual excitement due to the tantric influence of his subtle being or previous birth. All these things also prove that the development of Kundalini is better in a cooperative and loving society. The lower Guna-dominated parts of the society increase the worldly power, which then combines with the higher Guna-dominated parts and increases its spiritual power. This is also a division of labour, as per the tradition of the body-country. A single part of the society cannot absorb the lower qualities (Rajogun and Tamogun) and the higher qualities (Sattvagun) at the same time and simultaneously. By adopting the lower qualities to manifest worldly power, the higher qualities that manifest spirituality are destroyed. Similarly, by resorting to the higher qualities that manifest spirituality, the lower qualities that manifest materialism are destroyed. Practical self-knowledge arises only from physicality which resides with higher qualities. This is also the principle of Tantra. That is why there should be a high level of love and cooperation between the social organs having low qualities and the social organs having high qualities. This exchange continues in a healthy society. Sometimes a person helps a person with higher qualities by supporting the lower qualities, then in time the same lower quality person accepts the higher qualities, and the higher quality person accepts the lower qualities, in order to repay each other's debt.

In a healthy society everyone has their own standards. Some's level is of Karma Yoga, some's level is of Gyan Yoga and some's is of Sexual Yoga. One should not hate any kind of spiritual level considering it inferior. Kundalini is strengthened through all three types of levels, although there is some external difference in the method of strengthening it. It becomes very strong through Karmayoga. By doing this, over time, the Karmayogi gets elevated and spontaneously becomes a Gyan Yogi. Through Gyan Yoga, Kundalini gets a lot of strength and it comes closer to the path of liberation. Then the Gyan Yogi again gets upgraded and becomes a Sex Yogi. Through sexual yoga, Kundalini gets the momentum of liberation and becomes awakened. Therefore, the person who, while being situated in Karmayoga, loves the Gyan Yogi or the Sex Yogi instead of having enmity with them, gets many favourable situations in his level of Gyan Yogi or Sex Yoga. Exactly the same thing happened with Premyogi Vajra. All people in the society are respected at different spiritual levels. Some people find one method suitable, and some others find others. Many people, after the Jnanayoga level, again attain the Karmayoga level, and then, with time, attain even higher levels of Karmayoga and Jnanayoga. Thus, many people complete only 1-2 cycles, others complete more, and so on. Many rare people, after achieving success in Gyan Yoga for the first time, remain engaged in strengthening it and become recluse-sanyasis. That is why there should not be discrimination between different levels, because the goal of all is the same. Similarly, there should be no discrimination between the different sects and religions built on these three basic paths. Complete materialism is also the lowest level of spirituality, if it remains under the guidance auf spirituality. As mentioned above, Premyogi Vajra was also under the influence of spirituality created by an old spiritual man during his studies in science. Although he was free to take decisions, he was not bound. He had willingly accepted the company of spirituality. It should happen like this only. Perhaps the main reason for people turning away from spiritualists is that they do not generate interest in their subject but force it. Moreover, perhaps lack of knowledge or inhumanity is the worst kind of standard which should be avoided. Except this lowest level, all the levels are progressive, and are supportive of each other. In any society where these different levels were separated from each other, there was a loss of spirituality in that society and blind materialism or inaction was promoted.

Just as a man is not much disturbed by the activities of strange people and strange places, but on the contrary feels it as a pleasure, in the same way a detached man always remains so, because for him everything is strange i.e. like a stranger. Now just look at the dehpurushas and their activities. All of them are both true and false, that is, they are strange; then how can men exactly like them and their activities exactly like them be completely true? They are both, meaning they are both true and false. That is why the concept of non-duality is the concept of the subtle bodily being, and the best too. Due to Dvaita, the worldly life of both (the bodily man and the detached man) continues, and through Advaita, the joy of liberation of both remains intact. Another name for this non-duality is non-attachment. Similarly, the principle of non-attachment also works behind changing place or travelling. Detachment is also the reason for deriving pleasure from humor and romance with other women. Self-enjoyment from fear and adventurous activities is also a product of detachment. "Parvatah Dooratah Ramyante" Means Mountains are beautiful from a distance, this Sanskrit saying also reflects the principle of non-attachment. The spiritual bliss that is achieved through studies, stories, fables, novels, legends and other incredible stories is also achieved through non-attachment to them. Even among non-attachment measures, Puranas in the original Sanskrit language seem to be the most successful, because the Sanskrit language ignites the fire of the mind, due to which the sensual material world is also felt within oneself, that is, the Kundalini becomes active. Then how one can have attachment to his mental form? Inclination towards others (external world) is called attachment and inclination towards oneself (mind/soul) is called love. The direct untruthfulness of the stories of the Puranas creates disinterest or detachment, and the indirect truthfulness maintains the interest in reading them.

If there was happiness in things and feelings, that is, in mental attitudes, then beautiful things or people would never seem bad to anyone. We get pleasure from any beautiful thing because it reminds us of old events, towards which it is natural to have disinterest, because they are indirect and old, like distant mountains and without any meaning, that is, they have become like strangers. The joy of love that is experienced through separation is also one of non-attachment. In the same way, non-attachment is also present with the actions of others, actions done as per advice or orders given by others, dutiful actions and difficult actions, as a source of spiritual bliss. The pleasure we get from arts like song, drama etc. and from reading, writing etc. is of non-attachment nature only; because the mind gets completely immersed in such activities, and it starts feeling like a stranger to itself. Similarly, one also gets the benefit of detachment from TV-film, video etc., theatre-movie etc. No matter how hard cinema actors try, they cannot make their acting look real. They can imitate reality completely, but cannot make the emotions and gestures completely realistic. Therefore, detachment is present in his artistic activities, like a subtle bodily being. In reality, cine artists are body-men only. In this way, we always carry within our bodies a host of cine artists.

Science subject seems dull because people start having truthful mind towards it, due to which attachment is created. Along with this, the feeling of detachment arising from closeness with Vedic-mythological men or with divine men like sages, gurus etc. automatically gets associated with science, due to which it starts appearing interesting again. Same thing happened with Premyogi Vajra also.

In Vedic rituals, deities are imagined as human beings with beautiful appearance and beautiful physique, who regulate the physical creation in the same way as the body-man controls the bodily creation. The basic purpose behind doing this is also to develop the skill of non-attachment. Just as detachment automatically arises after attaining enlightenment, in the same way enlightenment can also be achieved through detachment. This shows that the philosophy of physiology is very easy and beneficial for all the hardworking men, because there is no need to do any formality in it, but only to change one's perspective.

If there was permanent happiness only in the bizarre mental states, then the man addicted to them and the evildoer would definitely get it. If there was happiness without them, then even fools, unconscious people and drunkard men would get it. In fact, spiritual bliss lies only in the middle path, that is, in the Madhya Marg, that is, in non-attachment. Therefore, the aim of Shavid is not to eliminate mental states, but to make them experienced with non-duality. We have to accept all the emotions and deficiencies as they are, because they are companions of karma, and by getting rid of them, rational actions like the one of the body-man cannot be performed. We just have to live life with a nondualistic perspective and remain detached from them. A man's life is like an examination, in which one has to do both the assimilation and renunciation of mental tendencies simultaneously. This is possible only through nonduality like the body man. Just as a dam is needed to stop the river water flowing due to gravity and an electric motor etc. is needed to lift the water up against gravity, in the same way non-attachment is also needed to stop the attachment driven by ignorance. Means a mental dam has to be built, and the fallen attachment minded tendencies of old times have to be raised up with the pump of non-attachment. Just as when gravity is destroyed, there is no need for the above mentioned pump and force, in the same way, when ignorance is destroyed, non-attachment itself remains intact. After giving some thought to the mind, one immediately feels the benefit of detachment from the remembrance of Shavid.

Physiognomy-philosophers keep worshiping the subtle bodily beings every moment with infinite treatments, spontaneously, that is, unknowingly, that is, without any formalities, because the subtle bodily beings are not present somewhere far away, but in their own bodies. They bathe them with water from many water sources like river, pond, sea etc. and offer water to them in the form of Padya, Arghya, Achamaniya, Abhishek and Shuddhodak etc. Various types of incense are offered in the form of diverse and fragrant winds. Treat them with medicines. They are made to sit in many types of vehicles and are also taken around in palanquins. They accept their teachings through the auspicious words spoken by them. Hearing various auspicious words, we offer them stotras recited, sound of bells and conch shells and praise them. They are offered various types of dishes. Their aarti is performed with the lamp-light in the form of eyes. They entertain them with many types of human entertainments, exercises in the form of resolution and action and many other methods like yoga and enjoyment. In this way, all the human works and behaviour done by the philosophers of physiology are forms of worship of God. All the feelings of a man, which keep his work under control, are his mental tendencies, which the body man himself creates within himself, to control the body world. A man who understands this considers the subtle bodily beings as the doers and enjoyers and becomes free from the bondage of karma. In fact, we have been worshiping and serving this body since time immemorial. But we do not get sufficient benefit from it, because we do not have the knowledge of this, and if we have the knowledge then we do not hold it in our mind while believing strongly. This belief becomes stronger by the study of Shavid, due to which the belief also gets strengthened continuously. Due to this, we get the fruits of our efforts done in the past in a lump sum form in the form of Kundalini awakening. In this way we can see that the philosophers of physiology are completely like the Vedic-mythical men. From outside they may seem more practical and rationalistic, but from inside they are even more calm, equanimous and free. They are like the ocean raged by a storm, which is like the ocean on the outside, full of body and mind, full of playfulness and movement, but on the inside, it is also calm and stable like the same.

If due to some serious situation, the Shavid-Gnani feels self-confused despite trying his best, then after that state of Rajoguna, he regains his inner peace through his calm behaviour with Dvaita-advaita mix feel taught by the Shavid. In fact, according to Shavid, one can attain salvation only by performing rational actions, because it is through action that the dazzling state of mind emerges, towards which one gets the opportunity to implement the non-attachment shown by Shavid. This detachment is nothing but the witnessing of the Vedas or the witnessing of the Buddhists. This feeling of witnessing is also called being present in the moment. This means that just like the body man, attention is given to one's entire present state in an impartial and detached manner. One should not cling to any other state except the present self-state. Due to this, the problem will persist in the same way as a person's problem will persist if he jumps from one thorny tree to another thorny tree. Like a mere subtle bodily being, one has to become calm by becoming detached from the present state of the self. According to Shavid also, non-attachment towards the mind can be achieved only if attention is paid towards the mind. If attention is paid to a particular branch of the present state of the tree of the mind, attachment to that branch will arise, but if attention is paid to the entire tree of the mind simultaneously, it will be called witnessing, with which non-attachment automatically resides. This is clearly visible even in daily physical/gross activities that clinging to a particular feeling/object gives rise to attachment, whereas giving equal importance to all feelings/objects gives rise to non-attachment. What is the use of talking more about the lifestyle of the body men, because we already know all this, because whatever we men do, those body men also do. Dva suparna syuja sakhayah, samanam vriksham parishasvajate, tayorekah pippalam susvadati, anashnananyo abhicakasiti. In this Sanskrit vaidik shloka, Dva Suparna, meaning two birds, i.e. Purusha and Dehapurusha; Sayuja Sakhayaḥ, meaning close friends like twin brothers. Samanam vrikshaam parishasvajaate – reside on the same tree, i.e. the same physical body. Tayorekah Pipalam Susvadati – One of them, i.e. the man eats the fruit of the Peepal tree, i.e. becomes attached. Anashnnanyo Abhicakasheeti-Second, i.e. the subtle bodily being does not eat, but just keeps looking, i.e. remains unattached. The entire Shavid subject is contained in this one verse of the Upanishad.

For low level seekers and beginners of Sadhana, there does not seem to be any better option than Shavid. Shavid is also beneficial for higher level seekers, although for them it is not an option but a supplement. Through Dvaitadvaita, both the soul and the world are simultaneously and equally accomplished. Dvaitadvaita gradually evolves and itself transforms into complete Advaita, which leads to self-awareness. However, even in the times of complete non-dualism, the mental states should remain intact, because through them only the practice of complete non-dualism continues and it also keeps growing, otherwise without practice, the existing non-dualism also keeps on deteriorating, how can it progress further? . Because just as the sustenance of duality is the dispositions of mind, in the same way the sustenance of Advaita is also the dispositions of mind.

If the body-man had also become the form of Achidakaash means unconscious self-sky due to attachment like a man, then in the same way, to attain Sachchidananda means consciousness bliss, he would have definitely felt the physical world with attachment, so that such an accurate bodily subtle physical world would not have come into existence, or it would have been lost. For example, if the bodily-soldiers had fled due to fear of death, then who would have saved the body-country? This proves again that the subtle bodily beings are detached. The principle of Sadhana of Shavid is also that the man should blow the Shavid occasionally or whenever necessary, for a moment in the midst of flying thoughts, without disturbing other resolutions. Due to this, Shavid's attitude of detachment is firmly linked with those thoughts, and at the same time his worldly work is also not adversely affected.

Even when a man sees his death approaching due to some disease etc., he is not able to give up his work, because he needs liberation the most. This proves that quick salvation can be achieved only through action. Like a man, the instinct for security and food is visible even in the simplest objects and independent living beings, then why does a man develop an ego like a mountain? Exactly the same tendency is clearly visible in the biggest planets, stars, constellations and even the universe, which do not have even the slightest ego, then the man called Purusha, such a small piece of the universe, has such a big ego. Why does it take care? In fact, except the man's body, all other bodies like it are saved from ego only because of non-attachment. Ego enters a man only through the path of attachment. By the way, if one has to imitate, then it should be done only of the subtle bodily beings, because among the non-attached things, if there is anyone closest to the man or in other words, the completely detached man form, then it is the bodily person.

If the earth is reduced to the size of a man, then the men on it will become as small as the subtle bodily beings. According to Shavid, the social men who directly meditate on the Chidakash/formless God are mostly not successful, because due to the dullness of their mental tendencies, they are not able to easily perform the kind of detached actions full of humanity like those of the subtle bodily beings. . Just as the dualistic viewpoint is binding, in the same way physiology alone is also binding, but the philosophy of physiology is liberating. Vedic culture, especially science mixed with Vedic rituals, is as liberating as Shavid. It starts giving self-benefits within a moment. Shavid is not just an artificial or contemporary philosophy, but it is eternal and evergreen because it is based on the living tradition that has been going on since time immemorial. In this philosophy only those facts have been presented, which are naturally present in the body. Therefore, this philosophy is natural as well as scientific. It is scientific also because the help of science has been taken for its accomplishment. Shavid can be called a new philosophy as well as an old one. New because no help of any pre-made philosophy has been taken while making it, and old because this philosophy also matches with the pre-made philosophies. Whenever Premyogi Vajra kept the papers etc. related to this philosophy in his travel bag, he felt a divine tantric and spiritual power protecting him. It simply means that moulding and preserving the Shavid in the form of a beautiful book or other related symbols is very beneficial as per the modern Tantra. It seems that this method works in the same way as the mandalas and symbols of ancient tantras. Similarly, this Shavid can always be downloaded and kept on all your e-reading devices, so that its divine Tantric power remains available every moment. According to Buddhist philosophy, tantra mandalas are subtle and symbolic forms of the gross world. What mandala can be bigger than the body mandala, because in it the entire creation exists in its complete form? The physical body is created by God, and is alive, dynamic and made of strong flesh and bones, hence it is not inert and transitory like human-made bodies. The tantric body mandala always moves along with itself. There are many other benefits of this body mandala also. When a man comes to know that he has been worshiping the body since time immemorial, then within a moment he becomes free as a body man. Because we have been worshiping this non-dual body mandala since time immemorial, hence by having good knowledge of it, the results of the non-dual practice being done since time immemorial are achieved immediately and spontaneously, due to which Kundalini awakening or enlightenment can happen suddenly or even without delay. It is possible that also, at the time of death, when no comforting shelter is visible anywhere, one's own body in the form of Advaita mandala proves to be the best shelter, if it has already been strengthened by Shavid. Because man loves his body the most (with attachment), hence seeing Advaita in his own body through Shavid is most beneficial/liberating.

We have been worshiping this body mandala unknowingly since time immemorial, and will continue to do so until we become free, because the bodies of all living beings are equally the reflection of the universe. Therefore, the non-dual perspective that will be developed in us by worshiping the body in this human life will be remembered in a subtle form in our future births too, because in those lives too, we will be living in the same type living bodies as in this human body. For tantric sexual yoga, it is essential to have knowledge of physiology philosophy. When both the Yogi and the Yogini see their own and each other's bodies as non-dual tantric body mandalas, then both are filled with non-dual bliss. Similarly, when both of them, at the time of mutual union, become endowed with non-duality, then the non-dual body mandalas are automatically worshiped. According to the theory quoted in the book, the mental attitude or mind-set held during sexual intercourse multiplies, means that non-dual attitude gets strengthened intensely and liberates the person. With that non-dual feeling, Kundalini meditation happens automatically and spontaneously in the body mandalas. That Kundalini, with the help of sexual arousal and Yogabandhas, keeps oscillating continuously between the sex chakras and the brain chakras, due to which it gets strengthened and soon awakens. Consciousness-milk is obtained from ordinary sexual relations, by the daily activities of the multifaceted and confused mind; but through the mental concentration achieved through tantric sexual intercourse, the milk of consciousness is obtained from the developing Kundalini.

Kundalini is actually a mental form given to the physical man, means it is the form of a divine and supernatural man. In reality, Kundalini is not a serpent etc., rather it is a beautiful, supernatural and pure/deep mental picture in the form of a god/goddess, a guru or a lover-girlfriend (consort). This mental picture itself is indirectly called Kundalini; because asking to directly meditate on the best and prestigious forms of Guru, God etc., at the so-called lower place like Mooladhar; doesn't seem social/polite or practical in any way. This Kundalini is meditated on various points and chakras of the body. It simply means that Kundalini is nothing but a personified form and a life-character given to the body-man, because the conscious body-man is present everywhere in the body. The Kundalini-chitra (human form given to the Dehapurusha) on each chakra is where every body-man works, eats, drinks, rests, because in reality also, on each chakra, some subtle bodily beings are doing some work, and some other subtle bodily beings are doing some other work. All subtle bodily beings, being similar in form, are in the form of Kundalini. Kundalini meditation is especially done on the chakras because those chakras are the main places of activities of the body, where the body is most active with detachment, hence it is manifested most effectively there. Therefore, in the form of Kundalini, it is easiest to meditate on them there. Similarly, their meditation on clearly felt places of the body (joints and other places with spasms, strains etc. during yoga) is also facilitated for the same reason. This means that Kundalini Yogis are worshipers of the physical body or body men. The proximity of a tantric consort/relationship increases excitement and activity around the sexual organs, making it easier to meditate on the Kundalini-like body being there. With the presence of a Tantric Guru, this activity continues for a long time, because then the reproductive power is properly utilized for the maturity of the Kundalini and its upward movement rather than for the pleasure of gross physical intercourse. The subtle bodily beings of these productive organs are in the full mood of creating a new world, hence their non-dual activity is at its peak there. That is why Kundalini is most clear and pure in those sexual areas. As soon as the intensity of power on those procreative centres reduces due to the practice of yogic activities, they become relaxed, because that clear Kundalini goes to the brain along with the prana/mind which is the companion of it through the yogic bandhas. In a way, it can also be said that the power present there immediately goes to the brain along with the blood flow (highly active subtle bodies are present in the blood too), because that clear mental picture is actually being formed in the brain itself. Due to this, the Kundalini becomes alive in the brain, and the seeker experiences a state somewhat like Samadhi (short Samadhi/incomplete Kundalini awakening/ Kundalini activation), which is a less-blissful state (than the great blissful state of full awakening). Yoga-bandhas help in diverting blood flow from the sexual organs to the brain. Through Pranayama, the physical subtle beings get plenty of vital air/oxygen, and they become strong. This makes it easier for them to help concentrate. In fact, the same picture should be given to all the subtle bodily beings, even if they are doing different work in the subtle physical world of body, because all the subtle bodily beings are the same in their soul form. In the same way, all the object-feelings and emotions (emotions being the reflection and part of the objects, are no different from the external objects) should also be given the same form, because externally all the objects also have the form of different bodies having similar nondual subtle bodily beings. They exist in form (as we have proved in Shavid), although their actual form is only one/non-dual form. Yoga sage Patanjali also says that samadhi is possible only through concentrated meditation. In fact, Kundalini Yoga is the technical extension of Patanjali Yoga. Patanjali's Ashtangayoga is also really nothing special; but it is only the theorized, simplified, socialized and rule-bound passionate sexual love. For example, if a driver learns the technique of driving well in the beginning, he becomes a skilled driver; in the same way, if a Kundalini Yogi also learns the best technique of this Yoga in the beginning, then he soon becomes a skilled Yogi. In fact, Kundalini Yoga has been developed keeping in mind the convenience of worldly people, because their external senses are strong, hence they cannot meditate on Kundalini directly in the brain, hence they have to meditate on the chakras indirectly. It is like giving bitter medicine mixed with honey to a child. All human subtle bodily beings are worship-able, even if they are doing small work, because they are fully capable of performing all human activities with Dvaitadvaita. On every chakra of the body, the subtle humanoid beings keep performing every type of work. Some group of them do one thing, some group does something else. Some are situated while resting. Therefore, Kundalini can be meditated on any chakra, depending on the situation, while performing any type of work or while resting. If you can rotate the Kundalini methodically, then it is a very good thing, but if there is difficulty in the beginning, then there is no need to worry, because Kundalini meditation can be done directly on any chakra, because Kundalini actually helps the body. The human form given is the human form itself, not given artificially, and according to Shavid, the subtle humanoid body is already present everywhere. By the way, the benefit of lowering the same Kundalini to the lower chakras and rotating it again and again is that the already glowing Kundalini remains available to us continuously through the vital air circulation. Sometimes some chakra is more active, and sometimes others. Therefore, one should not remain entangled in a single chakra, because all the chakras keep making up for each other's deficiencies. The main criterion is the amount of attention. It is also said in Geeta that self-knowledge arises from the abundance of Sattva Guna. The word Kundalini is not mentioned anywhere in Geeta. Therefore, it is self-evident that the mental samadhi picture (being full of sattva guna) described by Patanjali is actually

Kundalini. Because kundalini is the ultimate embodiment of Sattva Guna, and it alone provides self-knowledge. Kundalini is nothing special, but it is just a long lasting focused mind. If, without awakening, the mind is concentrated on a particular form (say Kundalini) for a long time, then there does not seem to be any need for the awakening of Kundalini, as Premyogi Vajra experienced with the Kundalini of the form of the first goddess. Even among Buddhists, there is a practice of always meditating on a fixed object. That object has been given a special name, just like Kundalini. Everyone is provided some unique thing to meditate. In reality it is the same Kundalini, the only difference is in the name. The object and principle are the same in both the genres. That thing varies according to the interest, occupation etc. of different people. That object is visualized through continuous practice. In Hatha Yoga, the subject of Kundalini has been described physically, such as the number and position of the nadis, the number and position of the chakras, etc. This has been done so that even materialistic people can get attracted towards Kundalini Yoga. Such people understand the language of measurements better, because they are used to seeing from physical point of view. In fact, Kundalini Yoga is completely psychological. A Kundalini Yogi should always remain happy, because just as in the physical world, only happy people live their life in the most appropriate way, in the same way, in the body-society, which is the best society, its people also prove to be happy and cheerful.

The principle of involuntary sensation also works behind Kundalini Yoga. At the time of Kundalini Yoga, the Kundalini picture is superimposed on the sensations of the body and mind, by meditating the Kundalini on the chakras. During daytime public activities, when mental and physical sensations become somewhat awakened, the Kundalini associated with them also awakens automatically and spontaneously. I am not talking about full awakening here.

Many people start connecting Darwin's theory of evolution and physical physiology with Kundalini Yoga. Probably they do this so that modern day scientists also get inspired towards Kundalini Yoga. In reality this does not seem to be the case, as Kundalini Yoga is a purely psychological/spiritual path, with no special focus on materialism.

Premyogi Vajra studied many ancient and modern books related to Kundalini Yoga, but he did not find the real form of Kundalini shown anywhere. In ancient texts, it may have been kept mysterious due to the fear of misuse, but in today's era of modernity and openness, no question of esotericism arises. At some places it has been described as a serpent, at others as a flame-crest etc. It appears that something is being hidden. In fact, this is a description of its nature and qualities like lightness etc. Its actual form is a pure mental picture/support as described by Patanjali, strengthened through continuous yoga practice.

Along with Kundalini Yoga, the refuge of Shavid is also necessary because in the higher stage of Kundalini Yoga, the seeker mostly gets affected by mental confusion and mood swings. By practicing Shavid, he remains established in Dvaitadvaita, and thus remains safe from confusion or illusion. At the time when the Kundalini of Premyogi Vajra was surging, she kept getting the company of the Puranas through that spiritual old man. Those Puranas, combined with his study of science, became a kind of Shavid, due to which he remained safe from confusion and psychosis.

The mental picture which is more likely to emerge in the form of Kundalini keeps coming to mind again and again, even if there is no special attachment or association with that picture. That picture is especially of a well-known and loved man, who's all his actions and feelings are clear and well settled in his mind. That picture can be of a teacher, a friend, an elder, a lover of different sex/consort or a sexual lover, etc. One should meditate on that picture. With regular and continuous practice, the same picture then becomes Kundalini. That Kundalini then gets strengthened in the brain, awakens when it reaches its peak, and easily leads to self-knowledge. Any new picture, such as the picture of a deity etc., can also be selected, although in the beginning it may be relatively more difficult, because the colourful actions and feelings of those deities etc. are not imprinted in our mind. They do not sit in the same manner as our everyday human companions. By the way, by giving the deity the form of a physical person, the karmic feelings of the physical person can be imposed on the deity, which makes this task very easy. The more fruitful the mental picture of that man is, the more that man is free from attachment and duality, and the more mental attraction he generates. By this calculation, spiritual gurus and deities {especially those with a tantric consort (so that one also gets the benefit of sexual attraction) and in the form of a subtle bodily being} are most fruitful.

In fact, by some divine coincidence, Premyogi Vajra himself got the shelter of the natural copy of Ashtangayoga written by Patanjali. The first two pillars of Ashtanga Yoga, Yama and Niyama, were automatically perfected in him due to the spiritual and non-violent background of his family and social environment. When he used to do physical and mental work related to land, fields and animals with his family members, especially his grandfather, his third and fourth padas or angas, asanas and pranayama respectively were automatically accomplished. The inclusion of the fifth Pada Pratyahara in him arose from the association of his grandfather, who was a very self-satisfied and patient priest. He also got the sanskars means impressions of the sixth-seventh foot, dharana-meditation from him, because he used to do spiritual practice regularly. The same seed-culture or good sanskara transformed into love for that friendly child mentioned earlier. When that love transferred towards the goddess, sexual attraction also got added to it and it became intense and grew into that form of eighth stage i.e. Samadhi, the result of which was the dream-time momentary spiritual knowledge means self-realization.

Regarding the Tantra, one thing is worth noting here. Perhaps there has been a mistake in the general public's understanding of Patanjali's non-violence-dharma. In fact, the minor violence of Naishthik Tantric, which is done in the form of Panch-Makar (alcohol, meat, sex etc.), does not fall in the category of violence. Through it they are proving non-dual knowledge and self-knowledge, which are the biggest parameters of non-violence. If someone wears the garb of non-violence and is engrossed in dualism, then it will be considered a show of non-violence. Daily yoga practice is also necessary because we do a lot of physical work or exercise, but do very little mental exercise. Due to this, the balance gets disturbed, the mind becomes restless, and it starts jumping here and there like monkeys, due to which the possibility of loss increases. In fact, for a healthy and happy life, all three qualities should remain in equal and balanced state in the body. Due to excess Sattva Guna, sleep gets disturbed and daily activities start getting affected. More Rajoguna increases the possibility of rape, violence etc. Ignorance increases with more Tamas. That is why it seems necessary to do sexual yoga along with Kundalini Yoga, because with it along with the satogun, sufficient rajogun and tamogun are also maintained. In Tantra, consumption of Pancha-Makaras is prescribed only to compensate for the deficiency of Tamoguna, although it can be comparatively more difficult to handle the Tamoguna arising from it, hence in principle it should be done only under the supervision of a Guru. It is necessary to maintain non-attachment or non-duality towards the changing qualities, only then spiritual development also occurs, otherwise there is a possibility of spiritual loss due to duality. Similarly, Amish-yoga under Panchamkarayoga of Purnatantra means leftist tantra also works like sexyoga. Under ordinary circumstances, the power obtained from the consumption of flesh is used to nourish the various modes of mind, thereby increasing ignorance. But in Amishyoga, the power obtained from consuming Amish bhog means spiritual nonveg is used to nourish the one-pointed instinct i.e. Kundalini. This power is mainly obtained from the association with the complete non-dual subtle bodily beings present in it (especially, if it is maintained with a reality-filled means nondual feeling). However, unlike sexual yoga, it does not automatically provide Rajogun, hence there is a need to be continuously active in this yoga. This also gives miraculous results like sexual yoga, if the feeling of non-duality is maintained continuously. Like all the remedies of Tantra, it also works according to the principle of 'all or nothing', hence one needs to be very careful and in the company of a Guru. Similarly, inside the egg is present the Shavid mentioned dehdeshrajkumari means body-country-princess, who with her innate non-duality is fully equipped for the creation of the entire body-creation. Like Tao, it is constantly changing yet unchanging. Many spiritualists believe that knowledge comes from the continuous Sattva Guna while avoiding Rajo Guna and Tamo Guna. But, in reality, according to Tantra, without possessing all three gunas together with a non-duality, real, profound and self-evident Sattva guna cannot arise. Due to this, they continue to boast about their moderate level of Sattva Guna, and are unable to develop further. According to the book, although Premyogi Vajra himself remained in the Sattva Guna based diet and lifestyle, but as per the contemporary situation, he also had to have deep association with the powerful Rajo Guna and Tamo Guna, due to which his mind could not remain untouched. It is a different matter that due to the influence of family values, he remained non-dual towards those qualities. Only then was he able to enter into that dense Sattva Guna, due to which he attained that momentary spiritual knowledge.

The above Tantra-principles appear to be the Tantra-secrets of Lord Shiva, which became extinct with time. All these secrets seem to have been received from non-dual humanoid being only. In fact, we can consider him as the form of non-dual Shiva. The meaning of replacing the goat's head on the torso of King Daksh seems to be that a man can get power even from the subtle bodily beings in animal form, and by awakening his Kundalini from it, he can elevate his mind through it. The same mystery seems to be behind the Tantric sacrifice system. But it is not necessary that the company of subtle bodily beings is attained only in the sacrificial feast. Animal service provides even greater closeness. Premyogi Vajra, with due attention to the nondual subtle bodily beings, did a lot of animal service and treated sick animals. He used to take sacrificial food only in rare situations, that too when there was a special obstacle in the proper service/treatment of the animals and in the meditation of the subtle bodily beings present in his/their body, which could not be avoided by other ordinary methods. With this, everything became fine, and Premyogi Vajra started experiencing the growth of his Kundalini again. Similarly, when Lord Shiva was roaming in the space carrying the dead Parvati on his shoulders in the Yagya of Daksha, various body parts of the Goddess fell at different places, and those particular places ended up as Shaktipeeths. We have proved this in the Shavid book as to how those Shaktipeeths are connected with the body-beings.

It seems to be true that orgasm is also required for enlightenment, especially to initiate samadhi. Leaving aside samadhi, the spark of orgasm is necessary even to ignite the small fire of dharna-meditation. Due to the spark of orgasm, either the gross fire (physical world) remains burning in the form of gross connection, or the subtle fire (mental world) remains burning in the form of subtle and mental connection. Gross fire provides only material happiness, whereas subtle fire premvides enlightenment along with material happiness. There are many obstacles in the path of physical intercourse, such as social disorganization and transmission of sexually transmitted diseases, etc. There are no such obstacles in the way of subtle intercourse that is why intersexual jokes are quite famous in the world. Therefore, subtle sex is a wonderful artwork. This also protects physical and mental strength. This is a social and modern form of ancient tantra. If a man attains enlightenment without experiencing any sexual love, then he must have experienced it in his previous life or in previous births, or in his childhood due to intense female attraction and entitlement to female affection. By receiving it, she gets the experience of sexual attraction indirectly, because intense affection also has the power which compensates the lack of sexual attraction to a great extent. It seems that enlightenment is nothing else but the ultimate mental sexual love. Who can be more steadfast in mind than a sex lover? In most of the yogic compositions one is asked to concentrate forcefully on dull things like words, sun, light, flame, sky etc. Meditation can be achieved through practice, but it does not yield quick results. What could be a more interesting thing to concentrate on than a sexual lover? If the attention is focused on any other loving man like Guru Etc., then there is definitely a contribution of the sexual lover in that also, because the mental picture of the sexual lover gets connected with the mental picture of that loving man due to assimilation (the book's theory of sexual relationship). This is the hidden secret behind the companionship of a Tantric guru and a Tantric girlfriend (consort). What could be more attractive than a lively, loving, friendly and affectionate intersex friend? More than half the path of spiritual practice is covered by the mere company of such an interesting friend. If such a friend, like the body-man, is full of nonduality, then mutual attraction and mutual attention or meditation easily reaches its peak. The remaining path is covered spontaneously by the grace of a good sage/guru and with the help of a little spiritual practice, and self-knowledge is attained. Because samadhi cannot be established only through physical orgasm and even without mental orgasm, samadhi is almost impossible, hence the secondary tantric path of resorting to physical orgasm in a symbolic form seems to be the best. With Tantra, especially with the aforesaid Vishamavahi Tantra (in which the Kundalini carrier is someone else, and the Kundalini is someone else), Guru is also necessary because if Kundalini in the form of Guru is not settled in the mind, then due to the immense power of Tantra, useless, tempting and ignorant thoughts will be strengthened, which will lead to bondage; But if the Kundalini in the form of Guru resides in the mind, then with that power that Kundalini will continue to get strengthened, which will lead to liberation. In

Samavahi Tantra, the Guru prevents the violation of sexual boundaries, and keeps mental sexual ecstasy at a constant peak.

In fact, we can understand enlightenment well only through romance, not directly, because it is indescribable. If the picture of the consort remains constant in the mind for many years, then we will call it the best love relationship. But if along with the best love relationship, there is also detachment from the love partner, then we will call it the ultimate love relationship. Self-knowledge is also similar in effect to ultimate love. This means that after attaining enlightenment, even the best love is transformed into ultimate love. In a way, ultimate love may not always lead to a momentary experience of self-knowledge, but one can definitely experience the full effect of self-knowledge. It is entirely possible that due to its influence, that too may happen over time, because cause and effect keep generating each other. Goddess Meera also attained enlightenment through this supreme love. Kundalini Yoga also proves this ultimate love. There is confusion about self-knowledge due to the way in which love relationship and self-knowledge are viewed differently in the society. In fact these two areas are interconnected with each other.

As mentioned earlier, and in the explicit stated, the sexual organ and the brain are both paired. If the kundalini is meditated upon in the genital organ, in its sensation and expansion, then it runs to the brain on its own by the contraction back of the genital organ and illuminates there, and remains in the brain for a long time (at least a day). Similarly, according to the tantra, during the vajra wash, if the kundalini is meditated on in the vajra sensation, it suddenly becomes ignited.

According to the above principle of sexual yoga, along with sexual yoga, Guru is also very important because during the time of sexual yoga, due to the close association of Sadhguru, his life-biography gradually, automatically and spontaneously appears in the mind in the form of Kundalini of the sexual yogi. It is as it happens in the aforesaid heterogeneous or vishamvahi tantra (in this the Kundalini is different and the Kundalini carrier is different). The above is absolutely true that if the Guru is not with you, then the energy of sex yoga will be wasted in the form of a bunch of mischievous, useless and at times harmful thoughts. If at the same time the Guru is also non-dual, then along with the non-duality developed from the mental

picture (Kundalini) of his form, additional non-duality also develops; Due
to which one gets the great power which can achieve Kundalini awakening,
self-knowledge and liberation, all three together. Along with this, if the
philosophy of physiology is also taken together, then super Advaita is
achieved, and the proverb "icing on the cake" comes true. In reality Advaita,
Anand and Kundalini; these three live together, and keep enhancing each
other. According to the set goal, the five elements of Tantra (Maithuna,
Madya, Maas, Matsya and Mudra) can provide the world/sin as well as
liberation/Kundalini/virtue. To say that Vammargi-Tantra was created for
those people who were immersed in the material Panchamakaras, so that
they could gradually leave them, so that they too could attain liberation;
displays the tantra in a passive or minor or secondary form. But on the
contrary, in reality Tantra is the main means of attaining power, and is
better for everyone. Everything is possible only with power. The awakening
of Shakti/Kundalini is visible through this, not otherwise. After awakening
of Shakti, the seeker has less need for Panchamkaras, hence he stops using
them or reduces them considerably. The so-called modern beer-yoga and
Apsara-yoga also seem to be based on Tantric-yoga/Panchmakar-yoga.

Premyogi Vajra was also affected by inter-gender-inter-caste type love in
his early adolescence. That love was pure, mental, symbolic and tantric type.
The reason for Tantricism was, incidentally and indirectly (while serving
human purpose, such as in drama, stage etc., due to the indirect trend of
depiction of sexual postures etc.) between Premyogi Vajra and his girlfriend
(consort), like cine artistes Like or say like this; Sexual intercourse in a
completely pure, mental and virtuous form happens spontaneously, that is,
by chance and without any desire, which we can also call initiation in the
language of Tantra, i.e. the beginning of physical attraction. Therefore this
beginning was desire less, natural and devoid of ego. Then one day it was the
day of Tantra-based ordeal of Premyogi Vajra. He reached his class early that
day. He was alone in the class, sitting on a part of the benches placed around
the circular table in the middle of the room. Just then his girlfriend-consort
also entered the class. He became somewhat uncomfortable and sexually
aroused, due to which he could not even say anything. He placed his book
on the table and pretended to read something. Devirani was also in a similar
situation. She pretended to be bored and by some divine inspiration lay

down on her back on the table and started looking towards the ceiling, keeping her feet on the ground. Premyogi Vajra could not keep his eyes on her even for a moment because he was extremely aroused. With the expansion of the genitals, an extreme and unprecedented sexual orgasm (genital orgasm) occurred. He could clearly feel the blood circulation rushing towards his sexual organs. His vajra-excitement had spread throughout the body and had taken the form of a whole body orgasm. He could clearly hear his heart thumping loudly, the vibration of which was spreading throughout his body. He could clearly feel the sound of blood running in the blood vessels of his body. There was redness all over his body, especially his face. Due to the immense heat generated in his body, his body had become like a living ember. Due to high blood pressure, his brain was feeling heavy, pressurized and throbbing. The waves of orgasm were hitting her mind furiously. The mind was filled with waves of thoughts and choices, mainly from areas related to the goddess. There was enthusiasm and light everywhere in his mind. For the first time in his life, Premyogi Vajra was experiencing himself in such a highly expressed form. Wherever there was excitement, Premyogi Vajra could see a very clear and attractive form of the goddess. Even amidst the excitement and waves of the mind, the picture of the queen was present in a more clear and intense form than can be directly experienced even through the senses like eyes etc. Premyogi Vajra was experiencing a unique, divine, subtle and sensual pleasure. He did not let it appear in the slightest that he was excited or particularly impressed by all this. He was pretending to be completely calm. Due to fear of teacher coming to class, due to the good inspiration received from the mental image of that old and spiritual man, and the fear of being potentially implicated by the goddess, he refrained from violating the decorum. Then, due to some divine inspiration, Premyogi Vajra started putting some pressure on his mind to read and understand something in the book lying on the table. Due to this some other thoughts also started rising in his mind. Then suddenly the expansion of his sexual organs and their excitement subsided. Heart beat and blood circulation became normal. The trembling of Premyogi Vajra's body stopped, and he started taking normal, steady and long deep breaths. It felt as if the blood full of energy from the sexual organs had flowed to the brain. Along with the same blood, the picture of Devi Rani also came out from there and entered the brain, which means Kundalini had become active. The door to the secret of Tantrayoga had opened before Premyogi Vajra. Devirani also got up after about half a minute and started walking. Devirani was forever amazed and impressed by the self-control of Premyogi Vajra. After that, Premyogi Vajra started studying his textbooks with all his heart and without any tiredness. He was doing this under compulsion, so that the mental picture of Premyogini (the first goddess above) in the form of his Kundalini, could always remain in his mind and not descend from there, because after descending, that picture would lead to physical sexual arousal. It used to cause body orgasm, physical discomfort and erection. In this way, along with samadhi, his material progress also became stronger. Perhaps this is the secret hidden behind the simultaneous development of both physical and spiritual disciplines through Tantra.

In the above natural tantra, Premyogi Vajra mainly experienced only 3 chakras, where mostly the first Goddess Queen (Kundalini) used to reside. They were; Sexual chakra, heart chakra and brain chakra. Kundalini kept oscillating between these chakras. Other areas may have also contributed, but these 3 areas were the main ones. In fact, these three chakras were expressed almost simultaneously. It is possible that they appear one by one and with a gap of a few moments, that is why they appear together, because the mental picture cannot be experienced simultaneously at all three places. These three areas influenced each other, i.e. enhanced each other. In fact, the strong mental picture of the Tantric consort is called Tantric-Kundalini. After that, with the indirect and spontaneous grace of the Tantric Guru, that Kundalini became stronger day by day. To balance the mental picture of Devirani's form, ultimately to save Premyogi Vajra from violating the limits of public propriety, the picture of his Tantric Guru also used to dominate his mind. Now to Premyogi Vajra, that mental-relationship form samadhi seemed more clear, pleasurable and conscious than the physical sexual relation. In a way, mental sex had defeated physical sex. After that, although he had developed a lot of self-control, but complete self-control could be achieved only after attaining self-knowledge, when he would spontaneously reject even the highest sexual temptations, although his desire for tantric sex remained. That was not available to him due to unavailability of a qualified Guru. Premyogi Vajra's desire was to maintain tantric orgasmic samadhi with her in any way possible. When that relationship of Premyogi Vajra was formed automatically without any external effort, then what was the need for him to get into unnecessary entanglements? Although Premyogi Vajra was also indirectly insulted a lot. Indirectly or through some indications, many people considered him a fool because he kept a woman in his mind, did not say anything, did not do anything etc. Many close friends would even start talking about obscene things in a humorous manner, which Premyogi Vajra did not mind about, rather the mental Kundalini of the beloved would become stronger in him, although sexual excitement would also prevail in him, that's why he mostly avoided such things; Especially when sexual arousal started exceeding the limit, his breathing started becoming irregular, and he started feeling as if he was suffocated; Along with this, the activity/ brightness of thoughts started falling. Devirani, who had a sharp mind, could get a clue about his signals and gestures, although she too remained cautious rather than feeling bad, and also enjoyed mental pleasure as per Tantra, as was reflected in her sweet smile. Once she had even told Premyogi Vajra about this in minimal words and signs, full of love, excitement, sparkle, sweet smile/pleasure, laughing with pride and excitement, and like coaxing a child. He became very satisfied, happy and proud with that. Still, with the tricks of his friends, didn't budge. Anyway, Premyogi Vajra felt that through direct sexual contact, that possessive attraction would be eliminated and self-knowledge would not be achieved, because there are some disorders in the physicality, encountering which the mental picture gets blurred to some extent. When the mental form becomes more clear and pleasurable than the physical form, then what benefit can there be in embracing physical disorders? This principle is the principle of Kundalini Yoga. In Tantra, the mental form is strengthened with the help of the physical form, ignoring the physical form/disorders. By the way, a man with duality cannot ignore physical disorders that is why sexual yoga can be harmful for a man with duality. That is why before taking shelter of sexual yoga, the devotion to duality is strengthened by taking shelter vaf sex-free and basic Kundalini Yoga, Shavid, Puranas etc. Premyogi Vajra was in a state of dilemma at that time, hence he took the right decision due to self-motivation. That state of complete self-control could last only for 3-4 years after the momentary enlightenment that occurred over time. In fact, most of the effects of enlightenment last only for 3-4 years. During that time he is like a junior god. During that time he speaks correctly, writes correctly and does correctly. During that time, most of the things he deeply thinks, speaks and writes turn out to be true. Although he is above petty interests, and tries only for the welfare of the world, that too only if it is necessary. After that that divine influence gradually begins to wane. Then to maintain it to some extent, one has to take recourse to Dvaitadvaita scriptures (Shavid, Purana etc.) and/or Kundalini Yoga. If both methods are used together, the best effect remains. Premyogi Vajra had to take shelter only in Shavid, because Yoga was not prevalent at that time, and even Purana lovers were not visible to him far and wide. Shavid also seemed suitable to him because he himself was related to the health sector.

Premyogi Vajra, in the biographical company of the old spiritual man, kept getting more and more joy and progress from the day by day growth of Kundalini, because probably that Kundalini was getting strength from the proven tantric sexual power by being in the company of the said first goddess queen. Due to this, his curiosity about sexual intercourse also became weak/ desire less. But Devirani's mental thirst was probably not being quenched, because perhaps there was no Kundalini active in her mind, or it was active weakly, which she wanted to strengthen through tantric sex. Probably she was not getting the same support from a side by side knowledgeable lover as Premyogi Vajra was getting from that old man/guru. Perhaps that is why her Kundalini could not develop. Probably due to this reason, later on, some mental hatred type towards Premyogi Vajra developed in her, which Premyogi Vajra realized after momentary self-knowledge, otherwise self-knowledge would not have happened. This was also one of many favourable circumstances. Still, the mental picture of her strange, malicious and accusing face kept troubling Premyogi Vajra on and off for many years. By the way, Premyogi Vajra's detachment towards that goddess was also amazing. Despite loving her deeply and experiencing the daily trance of her beauty, he could never convince even himself that he loved her, much less could he convince others. He enjoyed sex almost completely, yet no one could ever point a finger at the sexual conduct of him and his consort. If that's not a surprise, what is? He had shown similar non-attachment skills towards the second goddess also. However, whether it is marital or any other love relationship, Yogi and Yogini should never have even the slightest attachment towards each other, only then a firm foundation of sexual yoga is prepared. In fact, it is essential to have non-attachment towards the physical form of the Tantric partner, otherwise all the attention shifts from the Kundalini of the mind to the physical body of the partner, due to which the mental Kundalini gets eroded.

Based on the experience of Premyogi Vajra, the full effect of enlightenment lasts only for a few moments in the person, that is, as long as the experience is happening. After that he feels that he has achieved everything, that is, he has become selfless, and due to this, non-attachment and non-duality automatically prevail in him. The experience of complete satisfaction and non-duality can be achieved even without self-knowledge, only by continuous study of Shavids/Puranas. The residual effect of enlightenment lasts only for about 3-4 years. During these years, he teaches well to adopt duality mixed non-dualism. On the basis of the experience of Premyogi Vajra, after enlightenment, the non-dual/duality-nonduality mix/ dvaitadvait like the body-man becomes strong. This means that it is the feeling of nonduality that is directly responsible for liberation, not self-knowledge, because as mentioned above, the direct effect of self-knowledge is mortal. It is the feeling of duality taught through self-knowledge that leads to liberation. A lover of gods goes to the world of gods, a lover of ghosts goes to the world of ghosts, a lover of humans goes to the world of humans and a lover of animals goes to the world of animals. Then where will he go who loves everything equally through Advaita? In fact he will be present everywhere simultaneously. This is possible only if he becomes Brahman, because Brahma is always present everywhere. This proves that the non-dual man becomes free. Therefore, a person desirous of liberation should remain bound to Dvaitadvaitashastra like Shavid, throughout his life, instead of running after enlightenment. In such a situation, if enlightenment is to happen, it happens on its own, because the more we run after enlightenment, the further it goes away. In fact, it is futile to imagine enlightenment because it cannot be imagined. Self-knowledge is a state like that of a crazy person, who in reality does not seem to have any kind of knowledge. Therefore it would be more appropriate to say self-awakening. By running after self-knowledge, monism also comes under threat. Only a rare person experiences Kundalini awakening or enlightenment so that they can understand the importance of Advaita and can explain it to others too. If a person leaves Advaita and runs towards Kundalini awakening or enlightenment; it would be a similar case in which a person leaves his study-oriented daily life and runs towards teaching, but loses both. Or it is such a case that a person, abandoning the golden land, considering the mountain peak shining with the redness of the sun as the golden peak, runs to attain it. When the aspirant comes to know very well that there are innumerable bodies and innumerable subtle bodily beings everywhere in the universe, then he does not become attached to his own body and the bodies of other living beings, due to which the question of his rebirth does not arise. At the time of Kundalini awakening, Premyogi Vajra was endowed with Advaita perspective arising from the influence of Shavid. He brought Kundalini down at that time because he did not see any specialty in it at that time. To him, the same form of his self which had the harmony of Advaita seemed better and more beneficial than the momentary glamor and high-low experiences. Still, light and darkness (world), to bow down to both easily and forever, Kundalini awakening is necessary. He did not feel any special pain in bringing down the Kundalini. It simply means that Shavidpremi does not even care about Kundalini awakening. This also proves that Advaita approach is bigger than Kundalini awakening, and is essential for liberation. Kundalini awakening only strengthens Advaita. In fact, both enlightenment and Kundalini awakening produce momentary, sharp and best kind of mentality. The mind keeps yearning for that level of mentality, and runs here and there in search of it. Apart from Advaita, he does not find any mentality more similar to it anywhere else. In this way he indirectly learns to continuously maintain the non-duality, which is essential for liberation. Due to that Advaita, his energy remains saved from getting wasted in useless activities and thoughts. Due to this, there remains a constant possibility of Kundalini awakening stronger than the next and previous ones. If you are unable to do anything, then the inner body man, like Lord Krishna, says, "Sarvdharmaan parityajya mamekam sharanam vraj, aham hi tvam sarvapaapebhyo mokshayishyami ma shuchah". This means that if you do not have knowledge of Tantra, Kundalini is not activated and you do not know how to do sexual yoga, then the only thing that should be done is that at the time of any love, especially sexual love, maintain control over your body and the body of your beloved (consort). Great subtle humanoid body-beings should be meditated at every place. Due to this, the non-dual viewpoint itself gets strengthened, and the Kundalini also starts becoming active.

Similarly, Kundalini awakening also produces non-attachment rather than providing any specific thing like liberation (because as above, it leads to belief that everything is within the mind and is one's own form), which leads to Advaita. That is why many Advaita Siddha men do not even aspire for Kundalini awakening and self-knowledge. They accept only the naturalness of Shavid, nothing else. They do not accept the existence of any special and achieved state of enlightenment, Kundalini awakening etc., then why would they give importance to it? Therefore, they do not desire such conditions. They actually get everything themselves. This means that everything is present in Shavid. There is no question in the mind of a lover of dehpurusha, there is only naturalness, and happiness. They are always happy in whatever self-attained state they are. They consider such special states to be the product of duality arising from mental confusion and consider them to be false. From their point of view, everything is non-dual, normal and natural, just like Shavid. From all these facts it appears that real religion, real welfare and real salvation is hidden in non-dualism.

In this way, the door of Tantric mystery was opened before Premyogi Vajra. Then the picture/Kundalini of the consort kept rotating on its own between his lower and upper chakras, due to which, after a few months of natural/spontaneous practice, it became stable in his mind in the form of samadhi. An old spiritual man in the company of Premyogi Vajra proved himself to be his natural tantric guru, because he was unknowingly performing tantric work as a peacemaker, that is, by channelling his sexual energy. He was preventing it from going above the risky limit. Due to this, that energy was not being wasted, but was going into the brain and nourishing and enhancing the Kundalini. Even with a momentary glance, Premyogi Vajra could see his Kundalini in the physical body of his mental consort. That Kundalini was nothing but the mental picture of his own Tantric Guru, that is, he had unknowingly given the form of his Tantric Guru to the body-man in the form of Tantradev, located in the body of his girlfriend (consort). In the same way, Premyogi Vajra used to see the mental picture of his consort (feminine Kundalini) in the form of the body-man of his Tantra Guru. The inclusion of both Kundalini in the mind of the love yogi Vajra became firm. One Kundalini was male form and the other female form. Those two kundalinis were amplifying each other. They were both like as in Tantric Buddhism/Buddhism the visualized deity and the tantra guru have their own consorts. In fact, the body man has the qualities of both male and female, but to reach that bigender form, we have to divide the body man into masculine-body man and feminine-body-man. These mutually attractive forms continue to enhance each other until they lead to the full attainment of the entire body-being (self-knowledge/nondual state). This is the tantric essence of physiological philosophy. From the growing mutual sexual attraction between the above two kundalinis, a great force arose intensely raising the kundalini of Premyogi Vajra to Sahasrara. Probably those two Kundalini rose together up to Sahasrara and there merged and transformed into enlightenment. Descending from the peak of transient self-knowledge, he had for a few moments become trapped with the mental image of his consort's main sakhi/she-friend that was with her fullness and splendour. That mental form was experienced very sharply, the rest of the background scene was very slow. This also strengthens the possibility that he may have taken off from the trance-like launching pad attached to the form of the consort, directly to the summit of enlightenment. Many years later, when Premyogi Vajra raised only Purusha-Kundalini/that old spiritual man form to Sahasrara with artificial kundalini yoga, he had to settle for only 10 moments/seconds of Samadhi, without enlightenment. He could not stabilize that samadhi, because there was no intersexual attraction among the kundalinis at that time, although he was taking the assistance of sexual intercourse to raise his male form kundalini. It is therefore proved that without full-fledged Tantra Yoga with mental romance between men and women, the experience of enlightenment full of full adventure is very difficult and impractical. This description is for understanding only. According to the scriptures, Kundalini appears to be feminine. Although it is kundalini Shakti that is feminine, mental kundalini image can be of any form.

As mentioned above, several times Premyogi Vajra tried to establish a tantric relationship with the second goddess by creating Kundalini in the form of a woman (the first goddess), but he did not succeed. This means that in Vishamvahi Tantra, effective intersexual attraction is generated only by creating Kundalini of the opposite sex with the tantric partner.

By some divine boon/blessing, the visualized tantric initiation was established between Premyogi Vajra and his tantric girlfriend (consort) right in their teenage years. From it, Premyogi Vajra was filled with the unprecedented brilliance of Tantrayoga. Surprisingly, the female friends of the tantric consort also behaved with Premyogi Vajra in the same manner as the mental consort, although with a little more indirectness. They were probably the same as the group of friends and kins etc. who followed the princess of Dehdesh described in Shavid. Impressed by the tantric brilliance of Premyogi Vajra, his guru also automatically started getting attracted towards him, and unknowingly gave him the fruits of his entire life's practice. Influenced by the light of the unique and masculine brilliance of that sadhana, Premyogi Vajra's consort also became mentally more attracted towards Premyogi Vajra. Due to this, the picture of Premyogini became stronger in the mind of Premyogi. As a result, impressed by the even greater brilliance of his consort reflected in the Premyogi Vajra, his guru became more attracted to him than before. In this way the sequence continued, and both Premyogi Vajra's guru and his tantric consort increased each other's expression in Premyogi Vajra's mind. With the presence of the old guru, Premyogi Vajra got the power of self-control, due to which he could avoid direct tantric sexual intercourse with his girlfriend (consort), and could maintain the mental sexual attraction with full intensity, due to which soon Premyogi Vajra would attain the power of self-control. Sampragyata samadhi (continuous residence of the beloved's picture in the mind) began to occur with the image of the consort in the mind. Then due to some divine plan of nature, Premyogi Vajra and his consort got separated. According to the theory of Patanjali-yoga, Premyogi Vajra reached Asamprajnata Samadhi (A = not, Sampragyata = abundantly known), i.e. connected with the beloved (consort), everything of Premyogi Vajra became weak and ineffective; this blissful and resolution-free state happened, within which that momentary spiritual knowledge was hidden. Everything of Premyogi Vajra was connected with his beloved, even his own mind and soul. Therefore he himself became void. That emptiness was virtual. In reality, everything was there, but it was like nothingness. Probably it is a state of great detachment called parvairagya and great nonduality. In fact, many people do the work of getting their beloved (consort) in their mind, like Premyogi Vajra, but later they are not able to completely abandon her from their mind. For this reason they are unable to attain enlightenment. In other words, they are unable to give up the illusion of Samprajnata Samadhi and attain the Asamprajnata Samadhi of complete renunciation, in which self-knowledge is hidden. In fact, they are not able to forget their girlfriend (consort) because they have loved her with attachment. This proves that even at the time of love, the company of non-dual saints like Shavid, Purana, Sadguru, Sadvriddha etc. has immense importance. This is in accordance with Tantra Siddhant.

At that time, Premyogi Vajra felt that it was necessary to have fear in the society. If he had no fear of the society, he would have violated the decorum, which would have disrupted the Sampragyaat Samadhi resulting from sexual attraction. Similarly, if there was no fear, there would not have been a separation between Premyogi Vajra and his mental consort (Premyogini), which would not have given rise to the asamprajnata samadhi (shunyatva samadhi) which brought about enlightenment to Premyogi Vajra. In the absence of favourable conditions created by the above fear, both the Yogi and the Yogini would have definitely shone physically, like the western people with free culture, although then there would have been no spiritual development for them, but probably spiritual loss.

Premyogi Vajra also felt that self-enlightening and intense mental sexual attraction would not have been possible if both Premyogi Vajra and Premyogini had not been at the entrance of adolescence. He also felt this would not have been possible if both of them had not been of almost the same age and had similar behaviour. That would not have been possible even if there had been a private conversation between them. That would not have been possible even if either of them had tasted direct sex in any form or at any time at a mature age. This would not have happened even if that level of close interaction had happened between them earlier also. That would not have happened even if both of them were not each other's soul mates and Shiva-Shakti (twin flame). That would not have happened even if the two were physically bound together. That would not have happened even if Premyogini had not taken a small initiative to establish indirect tantric initiation with Premyogi Vajra. That would not have happened even if Premyogi Vajra had hesitated in making the spontaneous initiation. This would not have happened even if Premyogi Vajra had allowed Premyogini to have even the slightest awareness of his direct involvement in the aforesaid tantric initiation. This would not have happened even if Premyogi vajra had done the Tantric initiation arrogantly and willingly. This would not have happened even if Prem Yogini had not been continuously increasing his attraction towards her with her expressions. This would not have happened even if Prem Yogini had not appeared to him to be very beautiful, intelligent, and cheerful and had attractive complexion. This would not have happened even if Premyogini had been angry with Premyogi Vajra even before he attained enlightenment. If that happens, the curse (badadua) of Premyogini would hit Premyogi Vajra, which would greatly hinder the attainment of momentary self-knowledge. It was good that Premyogi Vajra had to face his symbolic anger after momentary enlightenment. Even on the day when his teacher gave a pictorial description of reproductive organs and their functioning in the class, he was absent from the class due to some divine coincidence. If he had been present that day, the sexual attraction between him and the goddess would probably have diminished, which would have weakened the samadhi that leads to enlightenment. That would not have happened even if all the teachers had not given him proper support and guidance. This would not have happened even if Premyogi Vajra had not respected Premyogini deeply from his heart. That would not have happened even if Premyogi Vajra had not got the company of that old spiritual man. Due to their very close and cordial relationship, over time, the mental picture of that old spiritual man became the Kundalini of Premyogi Vajra. Probably that is why it is said that in Tantra there is a great need for a Guru. That old spiritual man (Grandfather) had himself and unknowingly become his Guru, due to which Premyogi Vajra could experience Kundalini awakening so quickly and easily, after only 20 years of glimpse enlightenment, without any special sadhana. The guru of Premyogi Vajra, that aforesaid old spiritual man had gone to heaven about 20 years before his Kundalini awakening. This means that meditation can also be done on those old Gurus, who may have been liberated from the mortal world many years ago, and can be awakened in the form of Kundalini. Converting a living person into Kundalini is successful only if there is detachment from his physical form, otherwise due to yogi's connection with his physical form, it becomes difficult to meditate on his pure mental form. Nevertheless, one can meditate upon the living Guru without any hesitation. That is why a feeling of reverence and respect is created for the Guru, so that attachment towards his physical form does not arise. Premyogi Vajra had rejected even the relationship with the physical form of the first goddess, only then he was able to attain Nityasamadhi in the form of the goddess in his mind, which helped him in attaining momentary spiritual knowledge. Although it is difficult to do so, it becomes easy with practice. It was only by the association of that old spiritual man/ guru that Premyogi Vajra was able to do that. In this way, we can see how many favourable circumstances are required to attain enlightenment in practical life, and how much the fruits of good deeds of many births, the blessings of Sadguru and the grace of God are also required; still, rational and auspicious efforts cannot be neglected. By the way, Shavid or Veda-Puranas only create favourable mental conditions, not physical conditions or those in very limited form. To adapt to the physical conditions, physical efforts will have to be made. Although Shavid is always beneficial to more or less extent, but it is most beneficial with physical efforts and favourable physical conditions. But it is most beneficial with physical efforts and favourable physical conditions.

After the separation, time passed, and he lived a blissful life with the help of the Kundalini, which exists as the mental images of the Goddess Queen and the old spiritual man. But after a long time, the love yogi Vajra forgot his Kundalini, the first goddess, the image of the goddess, and the image of the old spiritual man. That diminishing kundalini itself was encouraging him toward sexual yoga. He felt that the motivation was given to create a normal sexual relationship, because he was unfamiliar with sexual yoga. But he was unable to find a woman for fear of pregnancy and fear of society and culture. So he became attracted to the man to establish an intimate relationship, but protected by God's divine inspiration, meaning that remained symbolic. By this and by the strength of the Tantra Sutra written by the author, that Kundalini gained sufficient strength and was firmly re-established. Then by wearing Kundalini he became very efficient till his marriage. Then his wife, the goddess, the second goddess, strengthened that Kundalini. His kundalini was motivating and encouraging him to have sex, because with the thought of sex, his kundalini would light up. This suggests that in most people with intense sexual desire, the kundalini is active, or longing to be active, and it continues to motivate them to have sex, for its activation or awakening. Although most people do not understand this, and they do not get proper guidance, so that many of them, either become sexual offenders, or they cannot get the help of sex yoga itself, for kundalini awakening.

It is a strange paradox that Premyogi Vajra was able to attain sleep-bound momentary self-realization experience only through indirect sexual intercourse with the first goddess; whereas his Kundalini could be awakened only through direct sexual intercourse with the second goddess. It is also written in ancient Tantra that self-knowledge is most accessible through direct sex yoga. This means that sexual intercourse is necessary, whether indirect or direct. It is possible that through direct sexual intercourse with the first goddess, he would have attained full self-knowledge (long-lasting self-knowledge or self-knowledge in the waking state), but through indirect sexual union, he had to be satisfied with only momentary self-knowledge (dream time). Still, what is the need for direct sex, if the strongest samadhi can be achieved only through indirect sex? Along with direct sexual intercourse, many obstacles are also present, especially in the so-called modern civilized society, which can hinder the enlightenment. By the way, till date it has not been known or heard if anyone has attained complete enlightenment even in dreams. Nevertheless, in reality, dream-time enlightenment appears to be extremely effective, because bliss is achieved without the help of any external senses. That is why the uselessness of the senses for pleasure is most exposed in it. Still, in my own practice or for other people, the enlightenment of the awakened state seems to be more reliable. Most people consider the enlightenment of dream time to be just a dream. If his dream-time self-knowledge had been complete, then his desire for self-knowledge would not have remained intact. But his mind was not satisfied with that enlightenment, and he kept waiting for a second glimpse for a long time. It is possible that in the first case, he found direct sexual intercourse harmful for enlightenment because there were no tantric gurus available to teach him tantric sexual intercourse. It is theoretically true/ natural that tantric sex without yoga leads to spiritual degradation.

That aforementioned tantric initiation relationship (like the cinema artists) was also uniquely coincidental. Competitions etc. are going on in the school. In one such quiz-type competition related to marriage management and child management, the love yogi Vajra and his favourite partner prepared for a knowledge battle with a group of other intersex pairs. At the time of preparation, a dearly desired text on the subject was made available by the love yogi Vajra on her request. In a modern text of that public type, two measures to prevent the couples from bearing children were described with line drawings without erotic colors (one is the method of enveloping the vajra and the other is the method of covering bell with watery ointment). Perhaps this is what led to mutual sexual consent for the tender minds of both partners, whose mutual mental sexual attraction, accompanied by favourable conditions, soon touched the sky. That moment of mutual mental consensus is the moment of subtle direct tantric initiation between the two sides. From that moment onwards, sexual attraction continues to grow and strengthen until enlightened trance. Meanwhile, once, by an unknown self-motivation, Devi Rani had jokingly called the love yogi Vajra, the three-eyed one who opened the third eye had the potential to bring down misfortune. This also proves that they both descended as Shiva-Shakti/twin flame. It is a relationship of previous births, in which a perfect self-light splits into two imperfect lights of opposite sexes called yin and yang, which then continue to attract each other to become complete again. They actually see their full form inside each other. Most of the time they cannot form a physical relationship with each other, because the man sees his own form in his twin flame-consort, then what about a physical relationship with himself? They mostly meet and separate. They try to fulfil each other in their own form by their mere presence. It involves the awakening of the kundalini/soul, as happened with Premyogi Vajra. By indirectly calling the love-yogi Vajra Trinetradhari, Devirani was actually teasing him with love, that is, considering herself a materialist and a scientist, she was insulting his spiritual-like calm state with love. Prem Yogi Vajra was greatly inspired by this to prove himself spiritual. This proves that even non-spirituality, if accompanied by loving humor, proper method and tolerance, is also an ally of spirituality, because it continues to give momentum and right direction to spirituality. Even the loving yogi Vajra, once, when he had not received the strength of non-spirituality, from other non-spiritual men, because of their uncooperative attitude, he himself had to become a full-fledged karma yogi means virtually non-spiritual with nonduality like the dehapurusha. After a few years of practice, he found the spiritual strength he needed, and he was able to experience the aforementioned transient samadhi/kundalini awakening. At the time of his indirect love affairs and fleeting self-knowledge, the modern era of extreme progress had not yet begun. Because the consort's environment was urban that was somewhat more convenient to live. It should not be understood from this that enlightenment and samadhi are possible only in the ancient era, because Premyogi Vajra's complete experience of Pratyaksha tantric samadhi, as has been described earlier, happened only at the time when modernity was at its peak. At that time he was taking full advantage of the peak of technological modernity. Hence it is proved that the mixture of Shavid and Kundalini Yoga is the best spiritual practice for modern times. Shavid-abhyas and Kundalini Yoga, both work well together. Kundalini Yoga provides abundant vital air, which gives the mind the power to think. With that power of thinking, spiritual thinking also becomes easy and convenient. By practicing Shavidchintan, useless thinking also stops, due to which a lot of life force (thinking power) is saved, which is very necessary, because in today's era of chaos, there is always a lot of demand for power or energy. With the power of thinking with which work is carried out, the non-dualism shown by Shavid is also proved and contemplated.

Modern scientists who analyse enlightenment also prove that after excessive mental activity, when there is a sudden mental astonishment, the possibility of enlightenment increases. The greater the difference between the functioning of two opposite mental states, the greater is the possibility of enlightenment. Same thing happened with Premyogi Vajra also. What can be a greater mental activity than that Samprajnata Samadhi, in which the mental form of an object appears more clear and real than its physical form? Even after the separation of the first goddess, he could have maintained the mental trance of her form, but due to the rituals of the family and social environment, this did not happen, because in Sanatan culture, keeping another woman in one's mind is considered a sin. Vajra, who was in love with her, gave up even the hope of getting her, and he fell suddenly from the sky of complete mental activity into the pit of complete mental astonishment. In reality, Premyogi Vajra did not abandon anyone, rather that mental image abandoned him itself, just as a fruit ripens and falls from the tree on its own. Separation etc. are just external excuses. Everything happens automatically in the mind. The only job of the seeker is to maintain the meditation of Kundalini continuously, through regular and continuous sadhana. Like a fruit, Kundalini also gets ripe on its own and then falls automatically. It is the natural instinct of every living being to progress. The state of Purnasamadhi is the highest state of the present mind. Therefore, it is self-evident that the only state higher than Samadhi is that of enlightenment. In this way, no one can stop a person in samadhi from entering into enlightenment, there may be a difference in the time period. If we talk about falling from the sky of Samadhi into the pit of lack of mind, then that lack is not as dark and ignorant as physical lack. That pit is of the form of complete nonduality and complete non-attachment, like the body-man. That pit is full of light, bliss and peace. That pit is full of equality and free from lust. The only difference is that in the sky of samprajnata-samadhi, the Kundalini burns especially and with utmost intensity, but in the pit of asamprajnata-samadhi there is uniformity all around. That trough of asamprajnata samadhi is so beautiful because its underlying samprajnata samadhi is full of non-attachment. By this calculation, the conduct of Shavid is also like that of Samprajnata Samadhi, because in it also there is abundance of non-attachment. That is why the possibility of enlightenment increases greatly with the presence of samprajnata-samadhi in the company of Shavid or Puranas, as happened with Premyogi Vajra, because at the time of his samprajnata samadhi, he was in the company of his Purana-reading grandfather. The depth of samadhi is revealed by this difference between the sky and the pit. It is natural that the deeper the Samadhi, the deeper will be the blissful and void-like trough generated by its maturity. So we can see that in this way scientists also indirectly praise the glory of Samadhi. As far as regular and continuous practice is concerned, for this one has to take a vow of "do or die". No matter what dire circumstances arise, the practice of Sadhana has to be continued, of course in some special circumstances like illness etc. Sadhana should be done only for a relatively short period of time. Premyogi Vajra also had a genetic bone disease called ankylosing spondyloarthritis, with which regular exercise is most important to live a happy and long life. With this excuse also, Premyogi Vajra got the strength to do regular sadhana. All seekers should find some excuse like this. The mind becomes satisfied with the excuses and starts doing the related work happily. The result of renunciation is also achieved according to the principle of this terrible transition. In ancient times, sages and gurus used to ask kings to suddenly leave their kingdom and go to the forest to gain knowledge, due to which most of the times they attained enlightenment using this principle.

Nowadays, efforts are also made to achieve self-knowledge and Kundalini awakening through the use of drugs etc. This practice was prevalent even in ancient times, when innocent sages used to consume cannabis in the name of Lord Shiva. Probably, it motivates a person to concentrate continuously towards one thing which is most ingrained in his mind. For this reason it provides spiritual benefits. Although some particular thing or person must already be firmly seated in the mind, only then this method can be effective. It also has side effects, such as it impairs memory, thinking power, decision making power and power to work. Along with this, the brain's power to tolerate Kundalini awakening also gets weakened. At the time of Kundalini awakening, immense pressure is generated in the brain, to bear it for a reasonable period of time, it is absolutely essential to have a completely healthy brain strengthened by yoga practice. Actually, most of the seekers get a small glimpse of Kundalini awakening sooner or later. Now even their refined form is available in the market in the form of antidepressants, which if taken regularly for about one and a half months, transforms the person almost forever. That transformation is also similar to the transformation resulting from enlightenment and Kundalini awakening, although it is of a comparatively lower level and is accompanied by the above mentioned side effects. Like all the other statements in this book, I am writing this theoretical aspect also based on self-experience of Premyogi Vajra, because he too had taken anti-depressants for 35-40 days as per the doctor's advice.

If we take the natural state of Samadhi, then it is nothing special but a state of intense love. At the time of the above mentioned natural and indirect tantric samadhi of Premyogi Vajra, his entire body including his mind and brain had taken on the form of a consort. He could see his mental consort everywhere. In a way, Premyogi Vajra had completely taken the form of his consort. To people, from outside he appeared to be something else (man/premyogi vajra), but in reality, from inside he was something else (woman/consort). That tantric trance continued in his mind for many years, for about 2 years before the momentary self-realization and for 15-20 years after that. In fact, this is the definition of Samadhi, although it has many levels. In this, only the picture of Samadhi is always prominently present, everything else is secondary. We can also call this Samadhi as concentration or Ekagrata in Sanskrit/Hindi. At the time of that Samadhi, he was everyone's favourite and friend. There used to be a divine attraction and happiness all around him. In the beginning, during times of intense trance and sexual excitement, sometimes the first stream of his urine used to be of white colour. It meant that sexual secretion was being produced in abundance in him, but he was preserving it, due to which his sexual power was strengthening the Kundalini Samadhi in his brain, and some remaining white colour was being released as being discarded as a waste. Due to this, his sexual fluid was spread throughout his body along with the blood circulation, the lovely fragrance of which would emanate from his pores and spread all around. Domesticated animals (especially cows) were attracted to him and became extremely happy by repeatedly smelling and licking his body with affection. Showing the most special and silent love for him, the cows preferred to graze only where Premyogi Vajra was present. He himself used to smell himself many times and get engrossed in the deep bliss of samadhi. Probably this is what is called Ojas by sages.

Only the beauty of the goddess had settled in the mind of Premyogi Vajra. Hence, it is proved that self-knowledge is achieved through meditation of only one. It is also said, "Ek sadhe sab sadhe, sab sadhe sab jaye" means prove one, all other is proved itself. Therefore, even in Kundalini Yoga and Tantra Yoga, one should keep meditating on only one mental picture. That picture may have variations within itself, but the picture should be the same, the only one, like the goddess may sometimes appear to be laughing, sometimes in a serious posture, sometimes travelling, sometimes in solitude, sometimes in a crowd, etc. Similarly, the same Guru may be seen sometimes speaking, sometimes laughing, sometimes ploughing, sometimes pulling grass, sometimes doing worship, etc. Similarly, the same Shiva can be seen sometimes with Parvati, sometimes performing the Tandava dance, sometimes in Kailash, sometimes on a bull, sometimes in a happy posture, sometimes in angry forms etc. In Kundalini Yoga also, for each chakra, a seed mantra, a colour, a special state of a goddess and a special number of lotus petals have been given; that's just a subtle difference. They do not mean that the pictures keep changing, but that the same picture keeps changing forms with subtle variations, so as to avoid boredom. For example, on a particular Chakra, the Goddess can be seen wearing a particular colour of clothes, chanting a particular Bija Mantra, in a particular posture and seated with a particular lotus. Similarly, the same goddess remains on different chakras, only her expressions and related objects keep changing. Any person can give his beloved (consort) the form of Tantra-Devi. If someone meditates on the male form like Guru, Dev etc., he can meditate on him as a couple along with his secondary or virtual girlfriend (consort). With this, the visualization by the meditator will become simpler and deeper, due to the mutual sexual attraction between the two images. It may be possible that meditation becomes stronger with colors, seed mantras etc. By the way, Premyogi Vajra meditated only on his Guru, that spiritual old man (described in the dedication part of the book), in the form of Kundalini; with their various postures, states and life-characters; Ignoring all remaining formalities. Probably only then he could see him very quickly, in the form of awakened Kundalini (the aforesaid samadhi of 10 seconds). In fact, most of the people get entangled in the various formalities mentioned above, and remain deprived of the real and concentrated meditation, which is the main goal of Yoga. Perhaps these formalities were created only to teach meditation to the most foolish people of ancient times. For today's intelligent people, these formalities can only create confusion, in my opinion. Another belief also seems doubtful, according to which one has to practice each chakra one by one for several months. In fact, Premyogi Vajra used to meditate on all the chakras simultaneously in a single sitting, which is probably why he got quick results. Probably, only those seekers who want special power, keep meditating on the sole chakra for a long time. For example, on Vishuddhichakra, to attain divine speech and on Hridayachakra, to attain divine love. There seems to be so much power in sexual yoga that it can be easily practiced on all the chakras simultaneously.

With the change in Samadhi the mental personality also changes. Mental personality is the real personality, the body is just an appearance. Modern science calls such changing personality multiple personality disorder. This is just the kind of superficial talk that is made by calling an enlightened person insane. Nowadays, no one can know completely who is enlightened and who is not, no matter what scientific methods are used. This can be known only from the integrity and mutual trust prevalent in the society, as was the case mostly in ancient India. It is human nature not to believe in someone's self-knowledge. Lord Krishna also performed miraculous works, yet most of the people did not even consider him an ordinary wise person, but considered him only an ordinary or foolish cowherd's man. Earlier, most of the people, especially the Westerners and the scientific type, used to consider deep spiritual experiences like Kundalini awakening or enlightenment as mental defects or illusions, but now they too have understood that those experiences are not mental weakness but reflect mental acuity. Now those experiences are being proved to be true physically also.

The moulding of Premyogi Vajra's mind into the shape of his consort was possible only because of his natural and intense sexual attraction towards her. It was not just an empty sexual attraction, but it contained all the feelings and passions of love. Sexual attraction was like an additional force, which gave extreme strength to mental love, to the level of samadhi. He felt in her all the subtle feelings of love, such as motherly feelings, fatherhood feelings, wifely feelings, sisterly feelings, guru feelings, male-friendly feelings, female-friendly feelings, male-enemy feelings, female-enemy feelings, kindness feelings, violence feelings, non-violence feelings, goddess feelings, voluntary nature feeling, Emotion, feeling of abandonment, feeling of dedication, feeling of self-respect, feeling of respect/appreciation, feeling of concern, feeling of hard work, feeling of dedication/loyalty, feeling of scientist, feeling of materialism, feeling of spirituality, feeling of building the future, feeling of struggle of life/ Feeling of truth, feeling of intoxication, feeling of child, feeling of daughter, feeling of son, feeling of betrayal, feeling of unhappiness, feeling of happiness, feeling of humor, feeling of dependence, feeling of responsibility, feeling of obedience, feeling of attachment, feeling of non-attachment, feeling of duality, feeling of non-duality; emotion of anger, emotion of jealousy, emotion of shame, emotion of fear, emotion of sociality-anti-sociality, indigenous-foreign emotion, known-unknown emotion, cosmic-transcendental emotion, life-death emotion, feeling of happiness, emotion of sadness, emotion of boredom, leadership emotion etc. etc. It is surprising that he did not see any sense of hatred in her. He realized the faint feeling of hatred in her after his self-knowledge. It is possible that it may have had some partial influence earlier also, because the tree already exists in the seed. Anyway, the spirit of dualistic materialism will mostly hate the nondual spirit of enlightenment. How is the combination of fire and water? This also proves that for enlightenment it is necessary to attain all the senses, although with Advaita. Premyogi Vajra was fortunate that he got all the feelings so quickly, due to which he could maintain the non-dual feeling in his mind for a shorter period of time while that of being in the company of Premyogini, due to the constant company of his Guru. In a materialistic age, it may be difficult to hold on to nonduality for a long time, so one's spiritual development also depends on the time one takes to attain all the realizations. It is also surprising that Premyogi Vajra never conversed with her, did not even say a word to her, nor did he meet her alone, nor did he touch her or her things. This was the highest level of non-dual and complete mental love expressed by him that is why he did not feel sad even at her separation. Any type of love can lead to Kundalini awakening, although love mixed with planned design and tantric sexual attraction is most effective. Hence it is proved that everything is loving. Through that tantric love mixed with sexual attraction, a wonderful and cooperative friendship had arisen mentally between that rural love yogi Vajra and his urban girlfriend (consort), but nothing physically. Premyogi Vajra used to pass through nature every day while coming to his school. Hard work, discipline and humanity were prevalent in the school and its surrounding areas; because that area was located under the army. Together, it was also natural that animal violence (sacrifice as per Vedic rituals) also took place there, which probably combined with the spirituality there, gave rise to the Vedokta/Shavidokta Advaita prevailing there. Mixed with non-dual culture/spirituality, even minor humanity filled violence becomes benevolent. Premyogi was also surprised to experience Advaita there. There used to be lush green trees all around. There used to be quiet and innocent hill houses scattered far and wide. There was deep peace all around. Walking on the unpaved road for some distance, then coming down from it, passing through bright forests with rare and small trees and plants, crossing a rain fed drain and then climbing up to the part of the same road that cuts the bend of the valley-drain, and walking on it for some distance and repeating the same sequence 2-3 times further, was a part of his everyday life. Near the last stop of the roadside-journey, reaching home after climbing a very high and steep hill, on the other side of which is the lowest and somewhat flat peak, and after descending a little on a gentle slope, there on a wide path, Lord Shiva and the village deity being seen there in a grand temple; and then studying while helping the family members in the farm work was also included in that routine. While climbing that steep hill, he became friends with an old and small shopkeeper, who sells biscuits, toffee etc. in a small room made of mud and wood, right in front of the footpath built in the middle of the grass grown for animals. He used to be sitting with some stuff. He was of tall stature, medium build. He was full of fun and cheerful nature. There was a braid on his head and a big red tilak on his forehead. His shoulders were slightly bent. He used to wear simple type of kurta-pajama. The single-mindedness of yogis, i.e. the so-called ter in local language was also present in his nature, due to which his image in the society was also that of a mad devotee. Many people around him considered his uniform mental samadhi wave to be mental illness. He was also determined because he had also served in the army for some time. Seeing the child every day, elated with the power of mental tantra yoga and flying rapidly down the hill, he used to be afraid of the possibility of him getting hurt. One day he made Premyogi Vajra sit in his room and explained to him with love. Along with this, he also told him about the darshan given by Bhavani Mata and, turning his eyes a bit white, he got absorbed in meditation for a moment. Then he did not tell anything even when asked and by handing him 2-3 candies, coaxing him with love, he sent Premyogi Vajra on his way. Premyogi Vajra found them mysterious. It is possible that he too might have had some hand in the contemporary momentary spiritual knowledge of Premyogi Vajra. He preferred to travel on foot rather than by bus/vehicle, but due to fatigue he would sometimes or intermittently travel by bus. While walking, Premyogi Vajra often got the opportunity to share his experiences with different types of friends. All those friends also experienced the tantric waves of Premyogi Vajra, so they also used to appear happy and cheerful with him. All the scenes automatically became associated with the mental picture of his consort. The beauty and freedom of the mind of Premyogi Vajra, as created from the unique and joyful stories of the Puranas narrated by those old spiritual men, was being completely imposed on the consort, i.e. the consort had become the divine Apsara of the Puranas in his mind. Various types of music, combined with Devirani's nightingale-like melodious voice, provided confirmation to her mental picture in his mind. The beloved (consort) remained happy and cheerful even in the closed, dirty and suffocating environment of the alleys/drains of her city, for this reason Premyogi Vajra had once told his friend that she was a lotus of mud. The surprising thing is that Premyogi Vajra never talked to his consort directly, but he heard her loving words many times in student groups. Probably for this very reason, once in front of everyone he called Premyogi Vajra as Kamandalu wala Baba in a voice as sweet as a cuckoo, full of love and sweet/symbolic humor. By the way, at that time he also had a Kamandalu-like figure related to science in his hand. It is said that what comes out of one's mouth many times turns out to be true, because what was said to Premyogi Vajra also proved to be true in time, when he got the spiritual experiences of true Babas. However, just like the feelings of ordinary small-town dwellers, at times she also experienced the feeling of being imprisoned in the city, which would appear on her face in the form of a brief and momentary glimpse. At that time the tender mind of Premyogi Vajra was filled with extreme compassion, although with detachment. Through the mental friendship of Premyogi Vajra and his consort, it was as if everything had come together and become one. Village with city, spirituality with materialism/science, satogun with rajogun and tamogun, liberation with bondage, attachment with non-attachment, sensual indulgence with control of senses, authority/self-respect with surrender, hard work with rest, convenience with problem. Happiness mixed with sorrow, cleverness or intelligence with stupidity, beauty with ugliness, love with neglect, movement with calmness, and the mountains mixed with the plains, as if they had become completely one. Yin and Yang had become one. In this way, by embracing all opposites together, attachment to one's present state is destroyed; that (reality) had been experienced by Premyogi Vajra. Then Yin and Yang were increasing each other rapidly. In order to balance the yin energy (the Samadhi image of the goddess) that had taken up residence in his brain, Premyogi Vajra's yang energy (his own male personality) was increasing itself, so that Premyogi Vajra would not lose his male personality. Probably for her, the mental picture of her male guru or lover was growing in her mind. In fact, the real gender difference exists only in the mind. According to this, if the samadhi picture of someone's mind is male form, then that mind/person itself is also male form, otherwise female form. Many times, the Samadhi image of someone is a male form, and the second Samadhi image is a female form. Such mind/personality is mostly that of a Tantric. Similar was the condition of Premyogi Vajra's mind. Those old spiritual men were his male guru, and that first goddess was like his female guru. The Samadhi picture of both the Guru-forms was always present in his mind. Perhaps in a similar manner, Devirani's yin energy (her own feminine personality) was developing to balance the yang energy of Premyogi Vajra (the Samadhi image of Premyogi Vajra) that had taken up residence in Devirani's mind, so that she would not have lost her femininity and would not have lost her jenuine place in the society. Inside her, perhaps a samadhi picture of a female form is being formed in her mind, or like Premyogi Vajra's mind, a samadhi picture of both the genders is being formed. In this way, gradually a very great male energy (yang) had developed inside Premyogi Vajra and a very great female energy (yin) had developed inside Devirani. Both those energies were creating great attraction towards each other, due to which the tantric samadhi of Premyogi Vajra became stronger and more stable than the samadhi created by Kundalini awakening. In fact, the stronger the Yang/Yin energy, and the smaller the difference in depth between the two, the more intense is the attraction that is created between the two, leading to the stronger Tantric Samadhi. This Yin-Yang Yoga is also known as Apsara-Yoga at many places. Naturally, the mental samadhi created by a woman's form is highly desired in a man's mind that is why woman has been given beautiful form. A man is relatively more attracted towards sexuality because perhaps he derives more power from it than a woman. However, in Tantric science, that power of attraction has been used to bring about samadhi in the mental form of great men like gurus, deities etc., and no doubt with the help of their physical form. By applying Samadhi in the form of Guru, one gets double or more and intense results, because along with the non-dual spiritual power of the Guru, one also gets his true love.

Premyogi Vajra had certain special characteristics since childhood. At the young age of just 3 years, he, along with his parents, grandparents, great-grandparents and a distinguished host family consisting of his priest grandfather, had undertaken the pilgrimage of the Tri Dham (except fourth Dham in Uttarakhand), which was considered very difficult at that time. During that journey, very good and surprising examples of his devotion were seen at two-three places. As soon as he left the house, he started crying continuously, due to which everyone got worried, but as soon as he reached Haridwar, his crying miraculously stopped, and after that everything became fine. Similarly, he became seriously ill in the middle of the journey, but miraculously recovered. He had collected many shells on the seashore, which he kept offering to Lord Krishna while roaming around Dwarkadheesh and humming something with great love, releasing them with full-hearted Anjali. Seeing that scene, even the priests of that temple were surprised and got emotional. In Gaya, where cremation was going on continuously, and where that day the mortal remains of a fortunate lady, adorned like a queen, was being carried in a gold-studded palanquin, there he was lost during the mass bathing, and after searching, was at a short distance away on the sandy shore, bathing with joy and happiness in a little water-filled pit naked like a frog. Once his hand got stuck inside the train, in a hole in the floor under the seat, in such a strange way that it could not come out even after trying hard. Then some miraculous person came there and took his hand out with a mysterious tactic, which surprised everyone. Once at the age of about 10-12 years, when he was passing through a footpath at the foot of a high mountain with his uncle's wedding procession, he had a vision of an old deity sitting on a rocky platform. It is possible that he may be his guru from his previous life, who have become visible in his mind due to the influence of his previous life's sadhana. By the way, people used to offer flowers, leaves etc. on that stone, because a temple of a deity was built a little above it. All these things show the connection of the previous birth behind the momentary spiritual knowledge of Premyogi Vajra.

In fact, the mental sexual attraction between Premyogi Vajra and his consort did not arise suddenly. Right from birth, Premyogi Vajra felt himself to be something special and God-loving. It is possible that there may be influence of previous birth also. He had grown up with a distant orphan-like relative, only 2-3 years older than him and a mischievous child, who had been living at his home since his very childhood. He loved him very much. Along with love, false, dramatic and temporary fights also continued; but instead of decreasing, love kept increasing. Premyogi Vajra was more loved by the elders because of his seriousness, lack of agility and contented nature, although the other child was more hardworking and obedient. The behaviour of that mischievous child was thrilling. While grazing the cows in the forest, he used to be the leader of the children from nearby to remote areas, just as Balkrishna used to be the leader of the Gop-Gopis. Some feminine qualities like shyness etc. were also present in that child. He used to take food items like ghee, jaggery, coconut etc. from home mischievously and distribute them among those monkey friends. In return, he would make them dance on his fingers, make them graze his cows, make their animals fight with each other, make them wrestle and do many other small tricks, whatever he wanted. Sometimes he would even make them do bizarre and strange mischiefs. Sometimes he would take them along and attack the corn field situated on the top of a high hill. All those baby monkeys would fry them and eat them in the forest itself. Sometimes he would remove the fences from other people's pastures and let his cows enter them and would himself go somewhere far away. Sometimes, while coming to school, he would steal bananas from the gardens of people who had gone out of their homes. Premyogi Vajra would keep watching and listening to all his pastimes with excitement and would also thrill others by narrating them. He was also very fond of women, and many times he used to make big jokes with them while playing. He was very fit, playful, strong and clever; but mostly, lagged behind Premyogi Vajra in terms of intelligence. Premyogi Vajra kept creating such problems in the middle of his blind race that he remained shocked and shivered, unable to do anything. However, at that time, many people in the neighbourhood were suffering from love disease, including some cases of so-called incest. To the author, all that seems to be an invisible and subtle effect of the association of Tantric Premyogi Vajra. In this way, Premyogi Vajra's childhood days were mostly spent with laughter, games and adventures. Premyogi Vajra had to face many types of obstacles since birth, such as the family-bound outbreak of serious and congenital diseases, due to which one of his elder and a nearby younger sister had entered the free world. Most of the time it happens that people who touch the spiritual pinnacle in their life have faced many troubles and obstacles in their childhood, because evil spirits and enemy spirits never want the world be blessed. Many examples of this are available, such as the childhood life of Yogi Shri Gopikrishna. The entire responsibility of tolerating all and moving forward as a family kingpin had fallen on Premyogi Vajra. Similarly, Premyogi Vajra's depression caused due to various such type of reasons would disappear within a moment after seeing the agility of that mischievous child. The rituals of spiritual practice etc. were continuously present in the house of Premyogi Vajra, which he got as if free of cost. It was because of those values that his love for that naughty child was true and trance-like.

In this way, after living together for 10-15 years, Premyogi Vajra and his domestic friend were separated. That friend had moved towards his real home to live a stable, independent and carefree life. According to Patanjali-Yoga, due to that separation, the mind of Premyogi Vajra had become very calm. Most of the mental world of Premyogi Vajra, connected to that friendly child, had become almost void (existing with complete detachment/non-dualism), although the tantric force that would give rise to self-awakening could not arise in that asamprajnata-samadhi. In the midst of that same emotional void, he was introduced to his consort/the aforementioned first goddess. That consort appeared to him completely like that mischievous child. In this way, the Samadhi of Premyogi Vajra suddenly and unknowingly shifted from the child to the consort. Adi Shankaracharya has published the theory of transfer of samadhi in his commentary on Patanjali-Yoga Sutras. Best friend's like that mischievous child and that girlfriend (consort) are also called soul mates. That second samadhi of Premyogi Vajra had also received the intense tantric power of intersexual attraction, due to which it had ignited to a greater extent than before. By the way, the story of Premyogi Vajra coming in contact with his girlfriend (consort) is also interesting. Premyogi Vajra studied in some other school. One day in the class, a young teacher kicked and punched him severely. For the first time, Premyogi Vajra was beaten in this manner, that too by a teacher and without any concrete reason. Premyogi Vajra became dejected and after the examination of that class, he changed the school, where he got mentally introduced to his girlfriend (consort). Well, there were some other reasons also for leaving school. Premyogi Vajra considers the teacher who showed him the right and straight path to be the greatest guru.

Even in the matter of Guru, a situation of confusion persists. The object-feeling which settles in the mind is the Guru. What benefit can there be in creating a Guru by force, especially leaving aside the Guru who is already present in the mind? The awakening of Kundalini in the form of a Guru can happen only if the life history of the Guru is experienced thoroughly and from the heart. In such a situation, what Guru could be better than one's own grandfather? Most people leave the light of their homes and wander in the darkness outside. The same secret is hidden behind celebrating Shraddha. When people have the right to awaken the transcendental biography of their ancestors in the form of their Kundalini, then it is also their duty to show gratitude towards them. The method of expressing that gratitude is called Shraddha. Incarnate men like Shri Krishna, Shri Ram etc. also appear only to show their special and attractive life-character. If for liberating meditation, not life-character but only body-image was required, then why those incarnated men would have displayed their charming and attractive life-character and not only their beautiful face. For this very reason, there are places dedicated to the biographies of great men in some corner places of pilgrimage, where it is felt essential to visit. One benefit of resorting to such biographical images etc. related to people is that it helps in maintaining good and sustained concentration in their mind via passage of memory. That is why the biographies of the incarnations include almost every type of field, as for example Shri Krishna was proficient in all the sciences and arts. When 24 types of living and inanimate objects like pigeons, clouds etc. can be the Guru of Rishi Dattatreya, then why can't a human-like living body-being be our Guru? In reality, Guru is always available everywhere, one just need to open his eyes. Similarly, people make strange idols and do not pay attention to them. One gets some benefit of Advaita from them, but one does not get the full benefit of Samadhi, or one gets it very late and only with the help of favourable circumstances. Probably, that is why in most of the temples, along with the idols of gods, the idols of some related knowledgeable elders/leaders/incarnates with whom the concerned common people have spent their lives are also installed. This helps them concentrate better and also gives results quickly. Along with this, non-dual benefits are also obtained from them (especially if their actual life-character has also been non-dual and sinless) along with from other deities too. In this way, according to the principle of Shavid, Advaita and Kundalini keep reinforcing each other. According to this principle, the rule of pranayama and meditation etc. is made in between the Vedic rituals and ceremonies. Vedic activities strengthen the feeling of non-duality, due to which the Kundalini also gets strengthened. Kundalini gets additional strength through pranayama and meditation, because through them the attention gets concentrated on the Kundalini. If Shavid is also practiced along with those Vedic activities, then miraculous effects can be produced. If one wishes, one can make do with only Shavid. Pranayama and meditation are secondary in Vedic activities, whereas they are main in Kundalini Yoga practice. It also seems to be true that it is essential to have a Guru in life. In fact, whenever a feeling of non-duality prevails in the mind due to the meditation of Karmayoga of Shavid etc., then the picture of Guru keeps residing or getting strengthened in the temple of mind. This happens because those guru are also engrossed in Advaita Sadhana. At the same time, they are also near old age, having acquired all the experiences of life, so they are automatically detached. Anyone can be a teacher. There is a difference between a guru and a teacher. There is mostly only one Guru, but there can be many teachers. The same Guru also exists in the form of Kundalini of the seeker. Here the meaning of Kundalini is the most strong/clear/dear/repeatedly exposed mental picture. It is possible that the Guru may change after a long time, but there is only one Guru at a time, just as there is only one mind at a time. It is also possible that as mentioned above, two intersexual tantric images or many strong mental images are residing in the mind, which are mutually reinforcing each other, but among them only one is the main one at a time, like the main one was changing for Premyogi Vajra. At a time, the main mental picture was of that old spiritual man. The mental picture in the form of Premyogini was the strongest, but in reality it was an ally of the main mental picture and was providing strength to it. This was so because the physical form of Premyogi Vajra's main mental picture was extremely influential due to the power of his Advaita Sadhana, and Premyogi Vajra remained in the close proximity to him along with respect as for a Guru. Therefore, its mental counterpart continued to draw his mental power. This is the divine glory of the Guru. In fact, the dearest teacher and friend is called Guru. Guru is both a friend and a teacher simultaneously.

Although after attaining enlightenment, Premyogi Vajra was aware of his attaining enlightenment; but he was not able to keep it continuous, intense and practical. He remained inactive and helpless type. It was as if he had completely dedicated himself to the divine rules and regulations of nature. He felt that his spiritual knowledge could be completely strengthened only by having direct tantric relationship with his consort. At that time, he could not even find a perfect Tantric guru. Due to this and many other social, cultural, religious, family-bound, economic, personal and practical problems, when he could not see any clear and positive path in life; then he composed the philosophy of physiology. This vision dazzled the dark streets of Premyogi Vajra with light. After having momentary knowledge of the Self from the indirect consort, Premyogi Vajra felt only one shortcoming in himself. That is, it would have been better if the momentary spiritual knowledge had occurred in the waking state rather than in the dreaming state. Probably due to this deficiency, he had a strong desire to have a direct tantric relationship with his indirect consort, but there were many social constraints. Because the images of both his girlfriend (consort) and that old spiritual man were very strongly fixed in his mind, hence the possibility of getting samadhi in the form of that old spiritual man in his mind due to direct tantric relationship with his girlfriend (consort) was very strong. With that samadhi, his above mentioned lack of experience would be completed, because with it the non-duality of the momentary self-knowledge of his dream would be superimposed on the non-duality of the samadhi of his waking state, thus becoming more practical. In fact, that lack of Premyogi Vajra was filled after about 20-22 years, with the help of the second consort (in the form of that 10 second samadhi mentioned earlier).

During the study of science, when Premyogi Vajra would make the complex subject very clear and exciting by drawing colourful pictures, he would experience the strengthening of the Kundalini and its upward movement. This tradition of colourful pictures has been prevalent in Kundalini Yoga since ancient times. Similarly, while commuting every day, he also experienced the development of Kundalini due to the songs mainly that time prevalent filmy love songs being played inside the bus; and at the same time he became very excited, restrained and balanced. It simply means that music is beneficial after and in the beginning of Kundalini Yoga. During Kundalini Yoga, simply listening to music like classical ragas or music in other unfamiliar languages seems to be more beneficial, because such music does not create verbal interference that works against meditation. With the onset of Samadhi state, Premyogi Vajra's experiences related to all three periods of time means present, past and future, i.e. all types of experiences, started getting associated with Kundalini. Similarly, Samadhi also has different levels according to the intensity of meditation. The 10-second samadhi described in the earlier part of this book was actually full-fledged samadhi, which cannot be endured for long. It is also called awakening of Kundalini. Such Purnasamadhi is a lower form of enlightenment. Prior to dream-state enlightenment Premyogi remained in a strong tantric trance state for about a year, with the mental picture of the first goddess. During that one year, the first Devi Queen in the physical form also remained continuously available to Premyogi Vajra, although he never gave her any special importance directly, but with her help, he maintained his tantric samadhi made of her mental form. He allowed it to be strengthened in the brain by the automatically acquired indirect/mental tantra. After that both of them parted ways. Due to this, his Kundalini became weak and along with it, the three-time world connected to it also became weak. In this way, in less than a year, she and along with her the world associated with her became void while being in the company of those Kundalini Tantra Guru. There was complete blissful emptiness in the mind of Premyogi Vajra. That blissful emptiness could last for a few months, only due to the natural company of the Tantra Guru, otherwise it would have been destroyed by the attraction towards worldly illusions. That blissful emptiness was strange and supernatural, because the whole world was being experienced as before, but it was as if ineffectual and did not generate cravings. The experiences during that time were much more intense, clear and strong than the experiences of ordinary times, although they were not logical/dual, and were not desire generating either. There seemed to be similarity and unity in all the experiences.

In the midst of that emptiness, Premyogi Vajra had a glimpse enlightenment. He describes it in his own words like this, "I am dreaming in a sweet sleep that I am standing on a bridge over the river in the valley, about 200 meters below my house. I suddenly felt completely open and my dark soul suddenly became filled with light. It felt as if my soul had been freed from a bondage. It was as if the light of my mind had spread into my soul. I saw the water flowing in the river. It had the same appearance as usual, but it did not seem to me to be any different from my soul and the bridge. The bridge was also usual, but in experience it was no different from my soul and the river water. On the other side of the river, there was a mountain in front, its about 20 meters of debris had fallen several days ago due to continuous heavy rains, narrowing the river. Miraculously, it slid straight down, due to which all the trees and plants present on it were alive and safe. In the above divine, strange and enlightened dream; when I looked at it too, its experience was also not different. Then I saw the great sun shining in the sky. Its experience was like others', and even its shine was like everyone else's. This entire incident was experienced in just about 5-10 seconds. At that time I was filled with ecstasy. I got everything that is possible to get in that experience. For those few moments, it seemed as if I had become the king of the entire universe. In that experience night and day were as if united. In that experience, both love and hate were linked. This means that everything was present in that experience. It was a complete experience. In that ocean of full experience, it seemed as if waves were rising in the form of river, bridge, sun, mountain etc., which seemed to be not different from that only ocean of experience (soul). Next morning when I got up from the bed, I found myself complete, devoid of lust, stress-free, peaceful, blissful, desire-less, like a newborn child and I felt myself in my natural self. It felt as if I had now recognized myself as I truly am, and had completed the race of life that had been going on for an unknown period of time. It felt as if having wandered from home, I had reached my real home. That experience changed my life immediately, completely and positively".

Generally, our personality is like a television screen running in a dark room. In this illustration, the soul has been compared to a dark room, and the mind has been compared to a television/movie screen. In such a situation, there is a difference between the soul (dark room) and the mind (lighted television/movie screen). But when an electric bulb is lit in a dark room, then there does not appear to be any difference between the room (lit) and the television/movie screen (lit). Both of them appear to be identical beams of light. In the same way, when self-knowledge occurs, then light spreads in the dark soul (one's own self in a deep sleep-like state/inanimate state or in a state of deep depression without resolution and choice, that is our dark self). Due to this, both soul and mind appear to be the same form of light. Premyogi Vajra had the same experience. In reality, that light is not an ordinary light like the light of a room or television/movie screen, but is a light of supreme consciousness and bliss. The analogy is given only to explain. In this way, Brahma appeared to Premyogi Vajra to be exactly as described in the main and famous Sanskrit texts. In reality, all evil is experienced by us as our dark soul. Similarly, we experience all the good things in the form of our mental tendencies. In enlightenment, we experience our soul and mental states as one and the same. That is why, as mentioned above, one experiences that all the opposing emotions have come together in that experience. The basis of expression of any knowledge/thing/action/result is the mental states or mind-waves. At the time when the soul awakens, all the mental states are not separate from it, but appear to be its movements of different shapes and types, just like the different types of waves in the ocean. Those all whatever magnitude appear only the negligible fraction of the awakened soul. For this reason, Premyogi Vajra felt that he had achieved everything and had done everything.

Till date it has not been known that anyone attained complete enlightenment even in dreams. In fact, the complete and correct way of living life can be learned only after self-knowledge. Through self-knowledge a person becomes calm, wise and lovable. Most people look at enlightenment from a particular perspective, as if light and light everywhere, or bliss and bliss, or it has both, or it has all the qualities of positivity and consciousness.

The surprise comes when at the time of experiencing enlightenment, all the qualities, even the opposite qualities, appear together. There is light as well as darkness in it; there is joy as well as sorrow; there is positivity as well as negativity; there is consciousness, as well as inertia or non-consciousness etc. Everything is there in it. In reality, it can be achieved only through positivity, but one should not be attached to positivity, only then it can be achieved. Enlightenment is not so cheap that it can be achieved by sticking to a particular ideology. No one can provide it to any other person, but can only show the direction towards it. Self-knowledge is that to the self-ignorant as an elephant is to the blind. Some blind man holds the tail and describes the elephant as a pillar, while another holds the ears as a banana leaf. This belief is also prevalent that after attaining self-knowledge, a man comes to know everything about the world and the other world etc. and he acquires many powers. In reality nothing like this happens. He knows everything indirectly, not directly. He knows only himself, knows his true form, and also knows that everything is a reflection of his own form, nothing else. For example, Premyogi Vajra was vaguely reminded of the dazzling moment of spiritual enlightenment he felt while watching a hit movie in the theatre. In the same way, even through other dazzling worldly experiences, there was some slight influence of that momentary spiritual knowledge coming in him. He does not know the answer to any question, rather he is not curious to get answers about the false world, and that is, all his questions come to an end. There is no question even in the mind of a lover of Shavid. When everything happens in his own body, then what is the question? Anyway, he is a worshiper of great subtle bodily beings, in whom there is no question. Whatever happens automatically and humanly, he allows it to happen, and remains happy. This means that Shavid has power equivalent to enlightenment. There comes no any extraordinary or superhuman power in him. He remains a human being just like everyone else. Many times, what he says or thinks turns out to be true, not because he has the power to change the world, but because future events sometimes come to his mind indirectly (i.e. without his knowledge). Still, there is some doubt as to whether words come out of the mouth of an enlightened person automatically, regarding an event that will happen automatically in the future, or whether the words spoken by him become true in time? If Honi or destined were to prevail, then why would people yearn for the blessings of enlightened sages? Probably only then, without taking enmity with any human being, it has been said in the scriptures to be ready to serve all human beings. In this case, this proverb is also famous, "Don't know in what form, Narayan will be found". By the way, he is very tolerant and avoids saying anything, because it seems that even by speaking too much, the Kundalini which has gained strength gets weakened, especially by harmful words, although to awaken the Kundalini, there is a need of practicality and Advaita. One has to work and speak also. It is less weakened with expression of resolution through written medium. However, only when it is extreme, from his mouth or pen, without anger or disorder, few double meaning words can come out, which can benefit the one with a true heart and harm the one with a deceitful mind. He never makes small or selfish wishes, but only makes worldly or universal wishes for everyone's welfare. In fact, enlightenment is a kind of energy sink, which absorbs Kundalini energy. At the height of his Kundalini mixed mental energy, Premyogi Vajra joined spiritual based social media, and there he announced that he would definitely find out the secret of Kundalini. Due to the intense desire generated from it, his immense mental energy was saved from getting wasted in his useless talks or useless campaigns etc., and remained engaged in the rise of his Kundalini. Then with the passage of time, with the awakening of Kundalini, his accumulated Kundalini energy simultaneously came out. There is immense power in accumulated mental energy. Most of the things spoken at the time of its surge prove to be true, hence one has to be very careful. The release of that mental energy means that the stored energy has faded in front of the sight of the great Kundalini, just as a firefly fades in front of a lamp. Self-realization is even a bigger energy sink than Kundalini awakening. As it is greater than the awakened Kundalini, hence absorbs that too. The hyperactive Kundalini of the form of the first goddess was absorbed by the momentary spiritual knowledge of Premyogi Vajra. Devirani's Kundalini had devoured everything of Premyogi Vajra, then later Premyogi Vajra's enlightenment devoured her too. Although that enlightenment was incomplete and momentary, hence it could not completely eradicate Kundalini. Therefore, gradually the power of that Kundalini kept increasing, and it became fierce. To unleash or combat that power, the aforesaid world-loving monologue 'Shavid' spontaneously emerged from him. It was also possible that if he had not hastily unleashed the Kundalini Shakti through his powerful words and writings, it would have erupted in the form of complete self-knowledge over time, but nature had something else in store.

Through self-knowledge it is not completely known what is right and what is wrong. The only thing he knows with complete confidence is that one should take the side of humanity, not inhumanity. He can determine what humanity is and what inhumanity is, only on the basis of his limited intelligence and experience, due to which it is natural for there to be more or less variation in the level of determination. Such practical experiences gradually increase through worldly activities and experiences. An enlightened person only comes to know which way of working is appropriate and which is inappropriate. That is, he gets direct knowledge of the glory of proper viewpoint (non-attachment and nonduality/advaita). Similarly, enlightened people can be of any temperament. Nature and contemporary circumstances mostly determine personality, not self-knowledge. Although self-knowledge also has some impact, because between two people with similar external circumstances, the self-knowledgeable person has the superior nature.

There is also a common belief that all the sins of the enlightened person are forgiven. But this does not happen, because although he does not commit sinful acts, but even if he does it forcefully, his self-knowledge keeps on diminishing with greater intensity as he commits sinful acts. After complete self-enlightenment oblivion, he too becomes bound like the common man and becomes a partaker of the consequences of his sinful actions, though more quickly than others, because he has to suffer their consequences in full in his present life, due to the less possibility of his next birth. After attaining enlightenment, man does not believe in superficial social and religious systems, rather he considers humanity as religion and inhumanity as unrighteousness. However, in special circumstances, he also practices social rules to keep them effective and to give good inspiration to others. As Shri Krishna has written in the Gita, "Dharmasansthapanaarthay Sambhavami Yuge-Yuge", according to which he makes great efforts to establish the religion of humanity with great cleverness and tact, while remaining completely detached. He works only with the inspiration of others and to inspire others, with an empty heart/detachment, because he feels that he has achieved everything, and there is nothing left to do, and therefore his only task of keeping self-knowledge effective and increasing it through continuous yoga practice is left. Although an enlightened person does not reject appropriate and self-enlightened actions. Another misconception is prevalent that the enlightened one does not reveal his enlightenment to anyone. It's not like that. He definitely reveals it to His unique lover. In fact, it becomes difficult for him too to believe, because the ego of the enlightened person is so diminished that he appears to be the lowest of the lowly. It is a separate discussion whether that exclusive lover will be able to spread it further in the society or not, because he too will be able to spread it further only to his exclusive lover, possibly. In this way, only in a loving society can enlightenment be spread and remain stable. Self-knowledge is just another name for passionate love. Even the matters of the mind can be told only to one's deeply loving friend, after all the soul is much deeper and more mysterious than the mind. It has also been said, "Pothi padhe-padhe jag mua, Pandit bhaya na koi; dhai akhar prem ka padhe so pandit hoe means worlds die reading bigger and bigger books, but if one studies two and a half words of love, then he becomes a Pandit". By the way, Premyogi Vajra was also asked by a well-known spiritual person to keep that spiritual experience a secret. Perhaps his objective was that its announcement would not create any hindrance in his development and studies or pose any threat to his security. Yet, most of the time, before 20 years of enlightenment, most people are not able to tell others about their enlightenment unless a very deep lover pursues them with full love and devotion. That is why enlightenment is also called the jaggery of the dumb. Even Shri Gopi Krishna and Shri Raman Maharshi could not tell anything for 20 years. In the first 3 years, if someone pleases him from the heart or receives his blessings etc. types, then it seems certain that sooner or later he will attain enlightenment. Although this work is difficult, because the enlightened one knows the heart of his devotee more than himself own. After 20 years, no such divine power remains in him, because he has almost completely forgotten his actual emotional experience of enlightenment. At that time he can only give guidance, nothing else. Although self-knowledge can happen at any time, the most suitable age for self-knowledge is adolescence, especially if one gets the company of an experienced guru. At this age, responsibilities are the least, while power is the greatest. At this age, tantric sexual power is also available on most of the occasions.

Perhaps he does not tell others about his enlightenment because he gets indications that it is almost impossible for anyone to believe what he says, and people may even take his claim in the opposite direction. He fears that by this the importance/light of enlightenment will diminish. He does not want to let the importance of the most valuable thing be diminished by this kind of publicity. In reality no one can know himself. Knowledge is of another thing only. If someone says that he knows himself, he will be called mad. Therefore, through which mouth can the enlightened person say that he has come to know himself, because as soon as he says this, it becomes knowledge not of himself but of some other thing, that is, the knowledge of the self disappears from the experience for some time, due to which the ability to speak it and listen it becomes difficult. Both of them suffer loss rather than profit. The reason for not telling also seems to be that the people's conduct around him is ignorant, due to which if he tells the right thing, he may be considered arrogant, and his safety may also be in danger. The biggest reason seems to be that he himself does not know the method of achieving it, because it has become available to him naturally and spontaneously. If he has direct experience of the sadhana method, then he should tell and teach it to others, otherwise he may become a laughing stock.

After momentary enlightenment, he remained in a continuous and abundant samadhi without any effort for many years, with mental images of physical forms of his tantric master and his tantric consort in his mind. Considering himself one who has done everything, he was always immersed in devotion to God. Worldly activities continued as before, but now with ecstatic samadhi. Sometimes both the pictures remained in his mind. Sometimes they used to come and go one by one. Sometimes they came and went according to the situation, for example, in romantic-type and physical/scientific-type moments, the image of the consort was dominant and in the remaining periods, the image of the master was dominant. This means that two Kundalinis can co-exist in the brain, although only one can be awakened, due to its continuous practice, like the Kundalini described in this book in the form of a Guru was awakened in the mind of Premyogi Vajra. It was good that he made his mental Kundalini created in the form of Guru the main one, because probably it remains active for the whole life, the Kundalini in the form of girlfriend is probably limited to the youth of the seeker. After enlightenment, the samadhi picture remains constant in the mind, because the mind which has fallen from self-knowledge, considers the samadhi picture as the second stage consciousness after the super conscious-self-knowledge; therefore one automatically takes refuge in it. Similarly, when one samadhi is broken, the enlightened person spontaneously attains another samadhi, and if necessary, maintains it continuously through Kundalini Yoga.

In this way we can see that Premyogi Vajra got the support of a divine, indirect and self-enlightening tantra, either coincidentally or due to the influence of previous deeds. Premyogi Vajra remained saved from his degradation for 20 years due to the nondualistic concepts and efforts helped by Shavid etc., that is, he remained around the same state of enlightenment, although he could not rise any higher than his spiritual levels achieved in earlier times, even he could not touch his level of enlightenment. Although physically, he became relatively highly developed. Shavid indirectly helps Tantra Yoga, because it continues to maintain the perfect level of detachment that one should have towards the Tantric consort and sexual intercourse. In reality, sexual yoga is nothing special, but is just a spiritual transformation of sexual attraction. Then, with the divine inspiration arising from the accomplishment of Shavid, along with Kundalini Yoga Sadhana, he took the help of Pratyaksha Tantra and with the previously mentioned practice of kundalini yoga for less than a year, he experienced the aforesaid 10 seconds of Purnasamadhi.

In the indirect tantra of Premyogi Vajra that is without direct sexual contact a state of continuous meditation like Chirasamadhi was created in his mind. That meditation, even without the achievement of Purnasamadhi (Kundalini awakening), became strong because it arose from natural sexual attraction and was not forced through yoga practice. On the other hand, there was no sexual attraction in his Pratyaksha Tantra, hence he practiced Yoga forcefully (Hatha Yoga - stubborn yoga), due to which he experienced that complete and momentary Samadhi (Kundalini awakening) which, by its attractiveness, generates a state of continuous meditation like Chirasamadhi. Although he had already strengthened the Guru Kundalini with help of his beloved consort Kundalini, that is why over time it could easily become capable of awakening, and eventually became awakened. The state of continuous meditation means Chirasamadhi, which is the aim of both direct and indirect systems, is the same, which provides momentary spiritual knowledge over time. This means that externally, there is a difference between the two from the point of view of morality, internally both the tantras are similar. Indirect tantra is mostly successful because it gets more social recognition than direct tantra. The second reason is that many times excessive spiritual powers are obtained through Pratyakshatantra, which sometimes can lead to anti-social activities, especially in the spirit of revenge. This is the war of words between Gyan Yoga and Bhakti Yoga. A Gyan Yogi practices artificial yoga, and by awakening his Kundalini, attains the state of Samadhi, or in rare cases, possibly even without Samadhi, such as through Sakshikaran practice etc., he can merge the world in his mind. But a Bhakti Yogi does not awaken the Kundalini directly; but with natural, spontaneous and concentrated love, he constantly keeps the picture of his most beloved person, God etc. in his mind; That is, one attains the natural and spontaneous state of Samadhi. Although Bhakti Yoga is most pleasurable, it is attained only by a select few fortunate people, whereas Jnana Yoga can be practiced by everyone. Due to deep love relationship, Bhakti Yogis/Prem Yogis are filled with love and fill the world with love and joy, like Lord Shri Krishna. This also proves that the basic principles of Tantrayoga and Bhaktiyoga are the same, the only slight difference is that Bhaktiyogis practice pure love, whereas Tantrayogis also resort to sexual behaviour. In fact, the basic principle of all spiritual paths is the same, i.e. Samadhi (samprajnata and asamprajnata). On the other hand, Gyan Yogis appear dull from outside, and are mostly confined to themselves and their limited number of disciples. Premyogi Vajra demonstrated both these types of yoga in action.

In reality, Kundalini awakening (complete Samadhi) is not the final stage, but only the beginning of the so-called final stage of enlightenment. Gradually the world merges into Kundalini and eventually becomes zero. At the time of indirect Tantra, the Kundalini of Premyogi Vajra, due to intense sexual attraction, was highly active even without its waking up, hence by its intense activity, it provided momentary spiritual knowledge. At the time of Pratyaksha Tantra, his Kundalini had clearly awakened (the aforesaid Samadhi of 10 seconds). Lord Shri Krishna's statement in Srimad Bhagavad Gita that I can appear to any devotee in any of my forms, underlines the awakening of Kundalini. In fact, by meditating on any form of God, that form becomes Kundalini. With the help of Kundalini Yoga, meditation becomes much easier. When the same Kundalini gets awakened, then it is called God Darshan. There is such a description in the scriptures that liberation is definitely achieved by seeing God, this shows that after Kundalini awakening, enlightenment happens sooner or later.

At the time of Prem Yogi Vajra's transient self-knowledge, the Kundalini-bearer or kundalini nourisher was also the Goddess herself, and the Kundalini form was also she herself, that is, the Goddess strengthened the Kundalini of her own image in the mind of the Prem Yogi Vajra by indirect use of her reproductive power, till the unbroken samadhi of Premyogi Vajra. Those old spiritual men were Dvaitadvaitabhimukh by constant practice of Puranas, so they protected the love yogi Vajra from mental confusion, mental agitation, attachment and violation of sexual boundaries by their association, directly when physically alive as well as indirectly afterwards (as the Kundalini in the form of those old man's mental picture), even when after enlightenment the kundalini of the picture of the goddess had become quiet. But at the time of the latter said transient trance, another goddess (possibly Patnidevi/wife) was the kundalini carrier, and the aged spiritual man was as kundalini carried, means she was strengthening the different than her form Kundalini in the mind-temple of the loving yogi Vajra. Thus we can see that Tantra Yoga can work in two ways. According to the second method, there is no need to be attached to the external appearance and beauty of the goddess or worshipping or meditating upon it. If a goddess endowed with pleasing appearance, beauty and other qualities cannot be found, and it is difficult to transform the mental image reflected by her physical form into a permanent kundalini, she should help in awakening the kundalini of the mental image of the guru, deity etc. At the same time, under the influence of the growing Kundalini, gradually those unpleasant goddesses become also pleasant. Perhaps it is only in the indirect sexual tantra (not in the direct tantra) or in the direct tantra with a goddess who is pleasing to the mind other than the wife that the same goddess becomes both the carrier of the kundalini and the carried (means Kundalini) too. Premyogi Vajra, with the second goddess, experienced the aforementioned transient and complete samadhi. His mental connection with the divine colour and form of the first Goddess was so profound that the general samadhi of her form itself remained constant in the mind of the love yogi Vajra, so there was no need for complete samadhi for transient self-knowledge. Purna Samadhi is not perfection in itself, it is merely a base point in the form of attraction to maintain attention or concentration. If that attraction is self-existent, then what is the need for the base point of perfect trance? This means that the indirect/psychic tantra is more effective, but it requires a psychotic type although humanely goddess to generate attraction. At the same time, it requires a very high level of physical self-control/discipline/isolation and a qualified teacher. This also means that in Pratyaksa Tantra, the appearance of the Goddess does not have any special contribution, except for the health of the genitals and the simple knowledge of tantric technique, because in it the Kundalini is given the form of mental picture of Guru-Deity etc., and the Goddess only acts as Kundalini-carrier. A goddess with a very attractive appearance can even create obstacles in it, because she cannot even like to harbour the kundalini of someone else's form except her own appearance and youth, because of her ego. Due to by being constantly accompanied by her physical form, the mental Kundalini of her form cannot even be created. One meaning of this also emerges that in Pratyaksha Tantra, a goddess of favourable or attached nature is not as effective as a goddess of non-attachment or contrary to mind nature. Perhaps this is the felt and logical reason behind the so-called infatuation related to women. Due to excessive workload, feeling of insecurity and fickleness of mind, strangers seem to be more attractive, but only for a short period of time. Instead of getting spiritual benefit from them, one gets only loss. After solving these problems/obstacles, solitude seems to be the best and one's own spouse is also the best.

There is a lot of book knowledge nowadays in the form of Pratyaksa Tantra, especially in Western and Buddhist types of societies, but Prem Yogi Vajra has written his practice of Samadhikarak Pratyaksatantra in his own words as follows, "Then I started a sex yoga conference with that simple kundalini yoga practice. Most of the time I gave my consort a kiss and a hug while she was dressed. With the increasing proliferation of the genitals, I meditated on the masculine kundalini increasing its clarity. As soon as the stretching became unbearable and bindu feared slipping, I would place the root lock, and the vajra would immediately loosen and the kundalini would enter the brain. By this regular practice, the Kundalini in the brain is fixed. With this, the divine, steady and subtle bliss of Samadhi growing. We looked forward to a full sexual encounter, a stress-free situation and sufficient free time. Then at some time (albeit up to 2 hours after dinner, excluding the time of fatigue, the time of stupidity and the time of sleep), with full positive thoughts, love and respect for the Goddess and happy faces; with the full digambara wearing, leaving the haste; With Kundalini meditation, the arousal of both of us was methodically brought to its climax by various Kama-Shastra rituals and thoughts. The Kundalini meditation would be done one-on-one on all the chakras of the lover, with touch and yogic bandhas. By the root lock, meditation is made steady and lust is subdued. Then we would both sit in the Yabayuma seat (yab-yum) in an embracing posture and the vajra would be placed in the lotus. I would raise the kundalini through the root bandha from the root/base through the spinal pathway to the brain and then lower it through the locked-mouth path to all the front chakras of the lover, meditating on kundalini slightly in each chakra. From the lotus of the lover kundalini would enter into the vajra and then the second cycle would begin. Some processes are in reverse order, i.e. Kundalini is raised from the lover's spinal pathway and is lowered through my front Chakras. When it is tired of, the sexual partner is in a lying posture facing upwards. That companion feels thrill in his vajra by repeatedly entering it in the bell. Then he relaxes a little and elevates the excitement to his brain with the help of yoga bandha. Then that becomes shrunk. Then he repeats the above action again and again. The flying lock is particularly beneficial, gives stability, and is simple, easy, natural and more effective. Doing this over and over again until fatigue, the kundalini is firmly impressed in the brain that cause Kundalini awakening quickly. Like the Yogi, the consort also raises her kundalini from her sexual organs by yogic bandhas. The consort meditated on her own kundalini in the yogic processes. Similarly, the compound process was continued for 1 hour minimum. When the excitement was unbearable, the vajra would be removed from the lotus

and the kundalini would be pushed into the brain by the bandhas, so that
the excitement would automatically subside. Long and regular breaths were
held. Then the thunderbolt would enter the lotus again. During the initial
practice, the slippage point was unknown, but with some practice, expertise
was gained. Initially I was affected by minor sexually transmitted diseases,
but after that I wiped my diamond thoroughly at the end of sexual
intercourse with the best cleaning methods so that the diamond remained
healthy. I had read all the methods from tantric books, and many of the
steps I took from my inner inspiration. In this way, with just one month
of consistent practice every day, I reached the level of Purna Samadhi
(Kundalini Awakening). Throughout that whole month, outwardly I looked
like a sexually eccentric saint, but inwardly remained completely
concentrated, and in my body and in the body of my wife-goddess also,
my kundalini (body-man-like) was constantly visible to me, because the
body-men are located in every part of every body, in the hair, in the skin, in
the nails, in every secretion, and so on. I would embrace them at any time,
and stroke their feet with great affection, and begin to attach them to my
bosom. All those feelings of love and hospitality, not artificial, were genuine
and from the heart. Seeing my behaviour like that, they were surprised at
first, because such a divine relationship had never been formed between us
before, even sometimes our relationship was very bitter. Sensing Patnidevi's
interest, I also taught her sexual yoga. He also cooperated with me with
great love and hospitality. This made my Kundalini feel all the behaviour
I had with my wife, which made her very satisfied and strengthened, very
clear and alive. The ordinary meditation I applied under ordinary Kundalini
Yoga, became distinctive when I took the help of sexual yoga, and became
very sharp and clear for several days. Although very little physical energy
was being wasted, some extra energy and extra time was required, which was
suddenly fulfilled by some divine coincidence."

All the above with Premyogi Vajra was possible only by the grace of the
Goddess. The above description of Premyogi Vajra proves that at the time of
final development of Kundalini, a concentrated and intense force is required
instead of small one; which is possible only with complete dedication to
Kundalini and intense level of sexual yoga. In fact, the tantric consort is
treated like a goddess, and is always kept happy, with great love (Premyogi

Vajra even worshiped her lotus-form feet), because it is in the tantric-devi that is such a divine power, through which she can provide enlightenment in just one birth. Along with herself, the Goddess should also always strive for the Kundalini awakening and enlightenment of her lover (consort) too. Inspired by the above experience of Premyogi Vajra, the author also felt that under the busy worldly life, along with the regular practice of Kundalini Yoga, one should also keep strengthening the Kundalini with the help of sex yoga in between, otherwise the Kundalini becomes very weak. Due to this Kundalini Yoga gradually starts appearing boring and difficult. In fact, after doing Kundalini Yoga for some time, one starts losing interest in it, mostly it is not due to technical shortcomings, but due to not re-establishing Kundalini again and again through sexual yoga. Kundalini awakening through sexual yoga becomes possible only when one leaves the entanglements of worldly life and becomes dependent on Kundalini Yoga and sexual yoga only. But Kundalini should already be strengthened by worldly affairs and/or by ordinary Kundalini Yoga. Through sexual yoga she only gets the escape velocity required for awakening, nothing else special. By temporarily leaving the worldly entanglement, the life energy that is saved and increased is used in the proper nourishment and awakening of Kundalini rather than in the world.

After awakening the Kundalini, many times, the love yogi Vajra would often do the pranayama and yoga-asanas within the Kundalini yoga in the Digambara posture with his lover. Then doing the aforementioned sexual yoga; with which, the power of self-control, joy and meditation would be greatly increased. He had undergone circumcision to treat sexually transmitted infections and prevent them in the future. In fact, there are various infections of the genitals, especially the female genitals, the most prominent of which is yeast infection. To avoid that, it is necessary to pay attention to hygiene, and keep the genital areas constantly dry.

Even if one gets only a glimpse of the brightly shining Kundalini or Kundalini awakening through sex yoga, it is enough, because through this, the person can then pursue that glimpse through regular Kundalini Yoga Sadhana, and take it to the level of self-enlightening continuous samadhi. As the great tantric Acharya Shri Rajneesh has also said. Perhaps this development happens on its own with time, although with the added strength of regular yoga practice, it happens a little more quickly. Most often, sex yoga cannot be practiced continuously due to a variety of problematic reasons. Anyway, Kundalini awakening happens so quickly through sexual yoga that most of the time the practitioner of sexual yoga is not accustomed to tolerate it for more than a momentary glimpse. Perhaps, with proper prior preparation or practice several times, one can experience a longer duration Kundalini awakening. His statement also seems to be true that in reality sexual intercourse is done only for attaining Samadhi, but the common man is not aware of this. When a man is in a state of samadhi and is leading a normal life, his mind is not much distracted by the love of women. Therefore, it is also clear that the real purpose of attraction towards a woman is to attain the state of Samadhi. He says that most of the people do not know the real and spiritual art of having sex. He again says that this happens in the same way as drivers know how to drive a car, but they do not understand the intricacies behind it. From this it appears that for humans, the most important purpose of sex is to attain the state of Samadhi. His point also seems logical that there is good in sexual yoga, but there is evil in sexuality (sex related talks, funs, photos, videos etc.); because from the former side there is accumulation and proper utilization of power, whereas from the latter side there is wastage and misuse of power. The meaning of sexuality here is to try to look beautiful externally, to have external and false ego etc. That is, that sexuality or sexual thinking, in which there is no trance, comes in the category of sensuality/sexuality. True sexuality means Sexual thoughts along with Samadhi Bhava are actually indirect sexual yoga, because sexual thoughts and Samadhi Bhava keep reinforcing each other.

Sexual yoga is best done during the day while fully awake, because foolishness prevails at any part of the night, and there is a lack of self-control, although it can be done at night if the practice is strong. Similarly, Kundalini yoga for at least half an hour before sexual yoga reduces foolishness. It also increases mental awareness, self-control and meditation. Various formalities are there in ancient sexual yoga, such as need for the practice of ordinary kundalini yoga for ten years before starting sexual yoga, and following various seed mantras, colors, pictures, customs, festivals, etc. Sexual Yoga is simplified by Premyogi vajra. In this he meditated only on the man-form Kundalini (the mental picture of his revered grandfather), forgoing all other formalities. This led him to practice ordinary Kundalini yoga for a year and after that he attained his Kundalini awakening only through sexual yoga and Kundalini yoga practices joined for a month. Full self-control is required in sexual yoga regarding sexual discharge. In ancient times, if sexual discharge occurred spontaneously without self-control, the yogini was mostly considered to be at fault. That is why we considered the yogini to be the guru, because the role of the yogini in controlling male sexual discharge is more important. It is easy to superimpose the kundalini on the sexual discharge through the self-control on the sexual secretions, when its great power is taken up by the kundalini. Sexual discharge requires great mental and conscious energy. That energy is saved through sexual yoga and spent on nourishing the kundalini. This also provides sexual satisfaction without sexual discharge, and also strengthens the kundalini. This also prevents unnecessary erosion of physical strength. Similarly, even if pornographic scenes are seen or pornographic news is heard after sexual intercourse, they do not adversely affect the mind, that is, arousal does not arise in the mind and body. In fact, the entire mental energy has been spent on strengthening the Kundalini so that there is no energy left to cause disturbance. Possibly continuous and prolonged inhibition of sexual secretion is also harmful to the sexual organs. Therefore, it is likely that the ancient Tantra scriptures prescribed the emission of sexual discharges nearing the menstrual period of the yoginis. The period is probably said to be from one week before to one week counted from the day of the menstrual period bleeding phase start, as the chances of conception at this time are negligible. This is why this is the best time to learn sex yoga during sex yoga training or even when sex yogi is a beginner.

In ancient times, most people were afraid of sexual tantra; because in case of its failure, they were afraid of their chanting, penance, fasting, charity, pilgrimage and other religious activities getting diminished. Nowadays, most of the people do not do religious activities at all, and even if a few do, they do not do it in a rational manner and with proper meditation (especially on Kundalini), hence there is no possibility of the above mentioned fear. Besides, nowadays most of the people are without discretion, detachment and self-control; are flesh eaters and indulge in sexual promiscuity. In sexual yoga, a woman is considered highly revered like a guru and like a goddess, due to which the declining respect for women can be saved. This used to happen in ancient India, examples of which are many Shaktipeeths and many goddesses, but due to the turmoil and chaos that has continued since the middle Ages till today, that tradition now seems to be on the wane. It is clear from the above reasons that in today's time, whether there is success or failure in sexual yoga, there is benefit in both the cases. Even if it does not provide spirituality, it will definitely provide material progress, which is much in demand in the modern era. This proves that sexual yoga is most relevant in today's times.

Sexual Yoga remains best when the Yogi-Yogini pair, for many years, remains at their original place of residence with Dvaitadvaita like the Dehapurusha; are living a very busy, practical and hard-working life; Both should have knowledge of Shavid and Tantra secrets and both should be taking strength from Tantra Yoga; and believe in the theory of spiritual progress being achieved through sexual relations etc. Even if these secrets are indirectly known, or even if there is only firm belief in them, it still works in most cases. If you are practicing Kundalini Yoga, then it is even better, but Premyogi Vajra realized that with a non-dual life full of busyness like a subtle bodily being, it is somewhat difficult to do Kundalini Yoga regularly. Actually, this happens only due to lack of practice. Non-dual life behaviour also works like Kundalini Yoga. However, in non-dual worldly life, non-duality is continuously maintained mainly through Shavid/Puranas, Vedic rituals etc. but in Kundalini Yoga oriented life, non-dual feeling is maintained continuously mainly with the help of Kundalini. Actually, Kundalini is also necessary for non-dual life, otherwise without it one would not feel like living non-dual life. Therefore Kundalini should always be kept active. Kundalini itself provides the best kind of blissful mentality in the monotonous life of non-duality. However, despite living a non-dual life stubbornly and without Kundalini, with time some Kundalini automatically becomes active. Kundalini and Advaita keep enhancing each other. The possibility of activation and eventual awakening of Kundalini is highest only in a loving and united family/society. It is only in this type of society that deep relationships are formed with different types of people. Then with time, the mental picture of the physical form of some particular person emerges in the form of Kundalini in the mind of some fortunate person. Such a loving society existed in ancient India. That is why the culture of ancient India is unmatched till date. Then both of the above mentioned sex yogis should go on a stay for a few years to a quiet, nature-filled and spiritual place (husband and wife along with children, this also inculcates spiritual qualities in the children). There both of them feel stress free, calm, happy and devoted to each other. Then both of them should practice Kundalini Yoga regularly, and when the practice becomes firm, combine it with Sexual Yoga. In between, keep visiting places related to their Kundalini. All these measures increase the chances of Kundalini awakening. Probably, as mentioned above, if a non-dual, hard-working and restrained life is lived with the consort for a long time, then only with time, Kundalini gets awakened easily through sexual yoga with her. The reason for this is that Kundalini gets nourished by living a non-dual life for a long time. That most beloved Kundalini of the Tantric also keeps connecting with his Tantric girlfriend/Tantrikardhangini, who has been living with him for a long time. Therefore, with time, disturbing feelings of unfamiliarity, insecurity etc. do not arise towards her. Sex Yoga gives best results only if there is no fatigue, stress, mental defects, unnecessary frills, mismanagement, distorted timetable, sting of insult, social exclusion, unrest, unattractive environment; crooked and unloving neighbourliness; corrupt/ loveless and disruptive society; and disruptive factors like environmental pollution etc.

1-2 years before Kundalini awakening, Premyogi Vajra had started experiencing some strange things, such as heaviness in the head, feeling of pressure in the head, headache, weakening of physical strength, numbness in the body, especially in the hands, feeling trembling in the arms, doubt about one's health, change in personality, forgetfulness of the beloved; having strange and vivid dreams, getting hints of future events in dreams, having interviews with deceased great souls, etc. There was pressure in his head, especially when there were strong and harmful impulses of anger etc. in his mind. It seemed as if those inflammatory impulses were being suppressed by that pressure. By the way, some time back he had also taken antidepressant for about one and a half months. Even with that his anger had subsided completely. But how could that medicine have a lasting effect for many months or years? Probably, all those transformational symptoms were arising due to the weakening of his old Kundalini (the first goddess), to fill the void of which a new Kundalini (the old spiritual man) was emerging. Even to his better half (the second consort/wife), he seemed transformed. About a year before Kundalini awakening, Premyogi Vajra had seen in his dream that he sun was shining in twos at night; was looking very clear and godlike suns, which lit up the night. It was a strange night because there was both darkness and light together. In fact, he saw the Sun and the Moon together, and the brightness of the Moon also seemed equal to that of the Sun. That dream filled him with joy for many days. It was very hot that year. It is possible that dream may also be a sign of that. Sometime before that, he had seen Lord Shiva in a very clear form along with musical instruments and his attendants (all the musical sounds were also heard clearly), due to which there was peace in his mind for many days. 20 years ago, even after that moment of epiphany, he had some mysterious and vivid dreams. Once he saw that a huge crowd of people was climbing a hill in a row, and all its people were taking turns to look at some infinitesimal atom in a microscope in a cavernous room, and that they were feeling satisfied and happy considering the atom as God. It may be possible that he is referring to the body-person. Around him, once in the vast space, he saw the cosmic bodies flying in a strange and surprising way, along with which an invisible celestial man was also giving a verbal explanation in a surprising and mysterious way, such as "The story of the creation of the universe. In the beginning, the big planets used to move making the sound of (saay-saay)". That scene was also very clear and impressive. As mentioned above, among the symptoms before Kundalini awakening, he used to feel semi-conscious type (stunned type). His memory; mental and physical activity had reduced considerably. He felt as if his head was spinning. He felt as if he was drunk and was tired. It is possible that his physical disease (inflammatory disease) etc. may also contribute to these symptoms. But these symptoms also coincide with Kundalini activity and maturity. The biggest reality test is identified only through self-experience. In those 1-2 years, he was intensely experiencing his second Kundalini (that old man) along with a life of struggle and development with intense nonduality. Due to those symptoms, he visited hospitals, got a CT scan of his brain done and also got other physical tests done, although everything turned out to be fine. As per the doctor's advice, to maintain his physical strength, he started consuming non-vegetarian food occasionally, with Shavid inspired

Advaita approach (albeit about a year before Kundalini awakening, either by unknown self-inspiration or under the influence of Yoga Sadhana), he became a complete vegetarian. Eating non-vegetarian produced some Tamo Guna in him, although it not only strengthened his body and mind, but also strengthened his Kundalini. His Tamo Guna was itself suppressed by the thoughts of Shavid. He also realized that his minor sins arising out of consuming Amisha food were quickly destroyed by the body-harmful and body-harm-causing incidents occurring sporadically in his life, due to which he himself felt the burden of Tamoguna reducing suddenly. This also puts a question mark on the belief that only vegetarians' Kundalini can be awakened. Although Premyogi Vajra did not eat meat in any form until he attained momentary spiritual knowledge. The philosophers of physiology who insist on eating non-vegetarian food, even while eating non-vegetarian food, feel that they are eating indestructible non-dual subtle bodily beings only, who neither suffer nor die. This strongly strengthens his non-dual viewpoint. Some sins are definitely committed by him, and according to the principle of Karma-Phala, even though he is suffering the fruits of those sinful actions, the same non-duality prevails within him while being suffered, according to the principle of Bhava Samaaropan mentioned above. Due to this, their non-dual perspective increases at double the speed, and along with it, the Kundalini also increases, because non-dual perspective and Kundalini live together. It also appears that the relatively greater amount of worldly practicality present in ordinary men who eat meat arises from the indirect influence of those subtle fleshly-men. Premyogi Vajra also felt his Kundalini becoming balanced and strengthened by eating non-vegetarian food. Probably this happened as a result of the balanced nutrition of his body, the indirect influence of its fellow subtle citizens and the direct influence of Shavid (directly from Shavid-contemplation).

It is mentioned in the Yoga Shastras that through Kundalini Yoga, the sins committed in the past are also destroyed. In fact, the deeds (Prarabdha) which have determined the human life of this present life, those deeds are not destroyed but get calmed down only after giving their results (although their effect definitely gets reduced a lot). But the karmas which are lying in the accumulated state, in the subconscious mind, and which have not determined the next birth, can be completely diminished by Kundalini Yoga.

Karmas actually remain in the subconscious mind in the form of unexpressed seeds, as has been described at one place in Shavid. Due to the effect of Kundalini Yoga, when even the most latent soul becomes awakened in the form of Kundalini, then the other and lesser latent emotions (seeds of karma) also cannot remain asleep, but they also keep appearing in the form of strange scenes during dreams, due to which they are destroyed in the same way as a seed is destroyed after germinating. Because those accumulated karmas are not determined for the present birth, hence they are not able to grow even in the form of a fruit-bearing tree, but only germinate and get destroyed in the same way as unwanted weeds in the field etc. Even before Kundalini awakening, many accumulated karmas are destroyed through Kundalini Yoga. Apart from the dreams based on those Sanchitkarmabeejas, the Kundalini Yogi also keeps having many other types of dreams, such as dreams which give an idea of future events or which come due to various other reasons. Because in ancient times most of the people used to be Kundalini Yogis, hence at that time dreams which gave an idea of the future used to be prevalent, due to which dream science emerged.

Similarly, once the simple exercises become established, swing recitation, subtle energy yoga and clear light yoga can also be practiced. Based on the experience of Premyogi Vajra, these are rarely required. The main ones are Kundalini Yoga and Sexual Yoga. The above three practices are reputed among the advanced Tantric techniques. All these tantric practices are first done in simple forms, then as the practice becomes firm, they are done with sexual postures.

If the fall is an agarbhaka (non-progenitor) slip, then its subtle energy (the kundalini image imposed on it) is elevated to the brain in the upward direction from the vajra tip by yoga locks. This prevents bindu from falling. In fact, the kundalini picture itself is called the bindu. This causes a relatively smaller decline in physical energy, although a sudden increase in the maturity of kundalini energy (samadhi). In tantric sexual intercourse, the male sexual secretion is not blocked for a long time, but complete control is maintained in its emission. Most sexual secretions are emitted while yogini is in the non-progenitor phase. It is probably a tantric mystery on the basis of the worship of the Shivalinga (Shiva+linga), the half-woman god and Shivaparvati (Shiva-Shakti). Kundalini meditation at tip of the vajra is one of the wonderful arts of the tantra. The sensation in the lateral areas of the vajra-tip in sexual yoga causes a slippage of bindu. By meditating on the kundalini in that sensation, the slippage of that bindu is prevented. By this, Kundalini is highly nourished and also, there is fullness in sexual satisfaction. This should be done very slowly and on top of that, extreme caution should be exercised during Kundalini meditation there, otherwise there is a possibility of slippage. Mastery in this comes from great practice. Whenever the drop/bindu slip is too close, the movement of the vajra should be interrupted and the kundalini should be raised by the bandhas. Before full practice, the limit of ejaculation should not be touched, but the kundalini should be raised by feeling a slight sensation, and then becoming calm. The sensation of it, evoked by the vajra, produces a thrill in the whole body. The tantra specifies the protection of the bindu, because the vajra gets loosened for several days with the slipping of the bindu. This makes it not easy to meditate on the kundalini above that. When the kundalini is not nourished in the vajra itself, how can it be nourished in the brain, because it is from the vajra that the kundalini approaches the brain? In other words, the Kundalini enhancement device is flawed for a few days, which the body-men even restore, although it is not possible to compensate for the loss for some time.

In swing recitation, the tantric and his lover, bound in the yabayumasana, breathe in opposite orders. When the tantric breathes out, his lover breathes in and when he breathes in she breathes out. The breathing tantric conceives that his kundalini rises from his root and flows out through his nostril, which the lover draws with her breath and lowers it to her root. With the breath of the lover, that kundalini emerges from her root/base and flows out of her nostrils, which the tantric draws inwards with his breath and lowers it to his root base. Similarly, this sequence can be repeated countless times and at different speeds. The tantric lover also stands watching her kundalini oscillate between the two bodies in the same way. This process can be done for any cycle/period.

In subtle energy yoga/inner heat yoga, one should meditate on Kundalini performing Yagya at the navel chakra. This is also true, because the main work of the dehpurushas of the navel area is to cook food by lighting fire, through which the dehpurushas of the entire dehdesh are able to eat. All the resolutions of the mind are burnt in that fire. In reality, resolution is just a bundle of vital air, which is spent in inflaming that gastric fire. The air of resolution from Muladhar is pulled up by the suction of the fire above. That air then ignites the fire further located in the spine, at the height of the navel. Along with the high flame of that fire, that air of resolution also rises upward through the chakras of the spine and reaches the brain. There it becomes cold, hence heavy, and falls down through front chakras. From Muladhar it is then again pulled upwards by Agni at naval. In this way, after a few chakras, that air of resolution calms down. In this way all resolutions are pacified. Due to this, with the power of those resolutions, the human-shaped Kundalini gets strengthened while performing Yagya. There are only two main chakras in the sexual tantra, Muladhara and Sahasrara. The Kundalini of a high seeker keeps swinging continuously between the brain and the base. When Moolabandha/Uddiyanabandha is applied, it gets situated in the brain, and when Moolabandha/Uddiyanabandha is left loose, it again gets situated in Muladhara. That is why Kundalini has been compared to a serpent, which sometimes opens completely and raises its hood upward, and sometimes gets narrowed in a coil-like shape. Clear Light Yoga is the highest quality yoga. In this, all resolutions/worlds are merged into Chidakaash. The seeker can adapt these basic Tantric practices to some extent as per his need and suitability. The main objective and guiding point is to strengthen the Kundalini. All these sadhanas are first accomplished in pure yogic form, then by combining the same sadhana forms with tantric sexual intercourse, the power of full samadhi and enlightenment is achieved with intensity.

It is worth noting that only after nearly 20 years of diligent study and various physical activities and one year of simple Kundalini Yoga practice, Premyogi Vajra could achieve some success in sexual yoga. Due to the hard-working behaviour of Shavid, his Kundalini became almost uniform and with moderate clarity, something stable/permanent and continuous, whereas with ordinary Kundalini Yoga, it got clarity and firmness. She got immense strength through sexual yoga, and she reached the height of awakening. Without strengthening the Kundalini, direct tantric interaction can cause harm rather than benefit. Probably, sexual yoga should not be done without regular practice of Kundalini Yoga, because the pressure of excessive workload on the sexual organs is calmed down only by meditation of Kundalini on the sexual chakras. Kundalini Yoga can be done even without sexual yoga, but by doing so, it is difficult for a good householder to get complete success, although the people who are complete renunciates or sannyasis get success in it more easily, because due to the peace of their renunciation, they have the strength of meditation. Therefore, they require less external force like sexual intercourse for Kundalini ascension. In fact, for a householder, the completeness of Kundalini Yoga seems to lie in sexual yoga only. When Kundalini becomes mature enough through Dvaitadvaita approach and practice of Kundalini Yoga, then it automatically gets attracted towards Sexual Yoga to attain the escape velocity which takes itself to Sahasrara. Many times, at that time the Kundalini seeker appears like a common sex patient/sex addict/sex freak, although he is being inspired towards the true path by his Kundalini. If at that time he does not get the knowledge of appropriate sexual yoga/tantra or tantrashastra etc., then his Kundalini may become extremely weak due to ordinary sexual relations, or he may go astray and become a sexual offender. If Kundalini does not get the liberating momentum, then it can continue to hover in the body of the person without awakening throughout his life. This happens in the same way that due to lack of escape velocity in a spacecraft, it is unable to overcome the Earth's gravitational field and go above the Earth's orbit, and keeps wandering around the Earth's atmosphere. Kundalini is strengthened at the chakras through Kundalini Yoga. At the time of sexual yoga, the same Kundalini flares up like flames of fire and becomes extremely clear, due to which the noise of other useless thoughts also stops. This means that Kundalini Yoga acts as both a protective sphere that protects from sexual harm and a pump that raises the Kundalini. Possibly sexual intercourse works like an "all or nothing" situation. This means that if in this life, Kundalini is not awakened by one, then there is a possibility of self-harm (going to hell). However, if done properly, this yoga is much simpler than all other types of yoga, and success is also achieved quickly. The possibility of self-harm is greatly reduced if it is accompanied by the company of a Guru, if it is done with a vow of monogamy and if it is limited to only one wife or goddess. There is a fear of harm from sexual yoga probably because it makes the man feel like intoxicated. One becomes full of spiritual bliss and becomes non-dual (Trans state). Because of this, worldly qualities like loyalty, dedication, fighting spirit and responsibility are not manifested in him as much as they are in a common worldly/working person. Due to sex, some directly and some due to the excitement arising from it, there is always some weakness in a person. Therefore, if he is not able to awaken the Kundalini through sexual yoga, then he remains deprived of satisfactory worldly life as well as spirituality. Although he is better than those drug addicts and lazy people, who are not able to enjoy the spiritual colourfulness and also do not like the world. At the time of sexual intercourse without yoga, attention is paid intensely to different places of the body (sexual area, heart area, navel area, cervical area, brain area), along with exercise, so that the good and bad things of the mind are concentrated there. All emotions are felt intensely. But on the contrary, by meditating only on Kundalini in sex yoga, the power of all thoughts goes to that Kundalini only, and it becomes extremely strong. There is also a theory that the area where the mind is focused becomes stronger because the blood flow to that area increases. By the same principle, Kundalini Yoga mixed with Sexual Yoga strengthens the entire body, because the Kundalini Chakras (7 aforesaid Chakras) are the base points of the entire body. Similarly, in simple Kundalini Yoga also, Kundalini meditation is done on various chakras, along with exercises. Due to this the Kundalini becomes more clear and intense. This means that Kundalini Yoga is a variation of Sexual Yoga with somewhat lower power, but with somewhat higher sociality. Without sex yoga, only simple Kundalini Yoga or indirect Tantra or a combined form of both is especially for those who are unable to do sex yoga, such as the elderly, unwell, children, unmarried and celibate etc.

That impressive thrill of ordinary sexual intercourse, that enthusiasm of wanting to conquer the world, that feeling of great power and glory etc., all those divine experiences and activities which are considered to be the most wonderful and most pleasurable in all the worlds; all of them, due to the effect of sexual yoga, achieve manifold growth and also strengthen the Kundalini. Gradually positive changes start being felt through sexual yoga. There is freshness and enthusiasm in the mind. The enthusiasm to work and the dedication to work increases a lot. Yogi's cheerfulness starts increasing. He starts handling worldly matters with fun and happiness. Nothing affects his heart, that is, he does not feel bad about anything, he does not get angry, but remains happy with himself, because the knot of the heart is open in him. He becomes like a cool kid. The child is ignorant and inactive, but along with knowledge and action, child type fun is present in him. The clarity of Kundalini and the joy associated with it starts increasing. The smell of Kundalini also starts being felt. Then sometimes the voice of Kundalini also starts being experienced, in a very light and subtle form. The attractiveness of his personality increases. Along with his consort, other known and unknown people also start feeling love, affection and respect towards him. With this type of faithful sexual yoga, his Kundalini appears to be fully expressed and alive in his mind, and awakens at any time. In fact, without sexual yoga, the full pleasure and full benefit of sexual intercourse cannot be achieved. There is a direct and straight relationship between sexual chakras and the brain. Other chakras do not do the work of establishing Kundalini in the brain as quickly as the sexual chakra does. Sexual chakras are extremely energetic. Kundalini reaches the brain directly and instantly through the sexual chakras. Premyogi Vajra experienced all these directly, both during Pratyaksha Tantra and apratyaksha Tantra.

As mentioned above, when Premyogi Vajra started practicing Kundalini Yoga regularly after 20 years of intense, practical and diligent study of Shavid, he came close to success in about a year. This means that if one's human life, full of nonduality and non-attachment, is lived for a long time like a subtle bodily being, with complete readiness, diligence, rationality and joy, then the mind becomes completely satisfied with life, and there is a deep desire to live life in him. Having enjoyed the world fully, cravings for it do not remain suppressed. This also helps one to concentrate well on Kundalini Yoga, due to which one gets success quickly. Premyogi Vajra also realized that after practicing Karma Yoga with non-dual devotion in the midst of common worldliness for a long time (about an average of 15-20 years), if there is a change of residence (about an average of 1-4 years) happening, then while doing Kundalini Yoga and Sexual Yoga at a new place, the chances of Kundalini awakening increases significantly. That is why in ancient India, there was a tradition of becoming a Karmayogi throughout life and going to the forest for knowledge in the later part of life. It simply means that after a long time of being engaged in action, when a person becomes calm due to some reason, then his outward physical energy turns inward and becomes mental, and gives rise to the awakening of Kundalini. But this happens only when the person's Kundalini is already strengthened by the practice of Advaita, and after attaining peace, that person practices Kundalini Yoga, otherwise his introverted mental energy is not able to concentrate on the Kundalini, and it wanders here and there. It disintegrates and gets destroyed in one's thoughts/activities. Exactly the same thing happened with Premyogi Vajra. Same thing is happening nowadays also. Most of the people, tired and bored with materialism, are returning back to the nest of their mind, and this is the reason why cases of self-awakening are increasing nowadays.

There is a high possibility of confusion about sex yoga. In fact, it does not look like ordinary sexual intercourse, but quite the opposite. Sexual Yoga seems like spiritual activities like worship/chanting-penance/self-study/fasting (for Kundalini) etc. Many people mistakenly think of themselves as sexual yogis, but in reality, most of them are engaged in self-harming casual sexual intercourse. For sexual yoga, the mind of both the intersex yogis should be calm, fatigue-free, and stress-free, with adequate time-power available and with a clear mental samadhi picture (Kundalini). For both of them, the only objective of doing sexual yoga should be the awakening of Kundalini, which should be present in the mind every moment in any form. The general rules laid down by great Tantric experts and Tantric Shastras should be known, and they should also be followed. For example, keeping in mind the public decorum as mentioned above, women are considered to be worshiped like goddesses and no one's wife or daughter is made a consort, because they are considered as a part of the emotional property of others. As far as possible, other problems are addressed instead of changing the consort. In sexual yoga, only respectful and dignified thoughts, words and actions are used. The most loving, dignified and best method of Kundalini awakening is sexual yoga with the vow of monogamy, only by adopting which Premyogi Vajra quickly experienced Kundalini awakening. If such essential pre-formalities are not completed, there is a weakness in self-control, due to which there is a possibility of sexual intercourse turning into an ordinary or low level sexual relationship. Nevertheless, moderate sexual intercourse in any form has some benefit. In this, the person should be open minded and cheerful, one who can implement "Vasudhaiva Kutumbakam" in practical form; not narrow minded. While there is a sense of self-pity in sexual relations, there is a sense of self-respect in sexual yoga. While there is depression or lack of mentality in sexual relations, there is fullness of mentality in sexual yoga. While there is a feeling of hatred in the sexual relationship, there is not even an iota of hatred in sexual yoga, rather there is many times more love present in the sexual relationship. While in sexual relations there is a feeling of humiliating each other, in sexual yoga there is a feeling of respect for each other. In sexual relations, where only one's own happiness and convenience is given more importance, in sexual yoga, equal attention is given to each other's happiness and convenience. At the time of sexual intercourse, where the mind takes refuge in worldly things and illusions; at the time of sexual yoga, one takes refuge in a mind filled with concentrated meditation on Guru, Vedas, Puranas, Shastras, Shavid, Gods and Kundalini etc. While sexual relations increase negative and ignorant thinking, sexual yoga increases positive and knowledgeable thinking. While the temporary and illusory shine of the world increases after sexual intercourse, the permanent and stable shine of the soul increases after sexual yoga. Where sex leads to bondage, whereas sexual yoga leads to liberation. While sexual intercourse provides momentary benefits, sexual yoga union provides permanent benefits. While people start moving away from sexist because of hatred, people start getting attracted towards sex yogi because of love. While sexual relations give rise to ill-will, especially violent feelings, sexual yoga gives rise to harmony, especially non-violent feelings.

Emotionally, psychologically and physically, sexual yoga is similar to ordinary sex, although with differences in mental approach, set goals and physical mechanisms. In ordinary sexual relations, the worldly, attachment-full and dualistic attitude of common people is present; whereas in sexual yoga there is a non-attached and non-dual approach. Similarly, in ordinary sexual relations, general and worldly goals are in the mind, whereas in sexual yoga, the goal of Kundalini awakening is in the mind. Ordinary sexual relations are done according to the common secular method, while sexual intercourse is done with the classical method and with the classical limits. Similarly, in ordinary sexual relations, the sexual energy gets divided into many types of thoughts, whereas in sexual yoga, all the sexual energy ignites the same mental Kundalini picture, due to which the possibility of its awakening increases greatly.

The greater love one has for one's own children as compared to the children of other people is due to sexual intercourse. There is so much power in sexual intercourse that it generates so much affection and attraction towards one's sons who have come from strange worlds and species, even if they had been bitter enemies in the previous lives. Similarly, sexual intercourse has the power to manifest the invisible (latent) soul in the form of a child. When this same power is used to revive (awaken) the invisible Kundalini, then this simple sexual process gets transformed into effective sexual yoga. In this, sexual intercourse is done like Kundalini Yoga and Kundalini is meditated properly, due to which the dormant Kundalini gets awakened most quickly. According to the same principle of Tantra Yoga, on the occasion of religious marriage, the Vedas, Gods, Gurus, friends and relatives are duly honoured and remembered, so that the proper level of spirituality and materialism is maintained throughout the life. Probably, in ancient India, that is why a woman of interest to the Guru and the elders was married, so that that woman could strengthen the Kundalini of their form through Tantra Yoga. Through sexual intercourse, even bitter enemies become best friends. For this reason, it has proved to be the best weapon of politics since ancient times. Inter-marriage relationships aimed at political, economic, family, cultural and other class-related interests are also a part of this chain. Exceptionally, the unjust violence that occurs due to illicit relations is done out of anger, out of misguidance, in the name of teaching a lesson to the society, by force, by placing a stone on the heart and by going against nature. This is a completely unacceptable and condemnable act, because due to the influence of sexual intercourse, those violence become disgusting, and as a result, the sins arising from them also increase manifold. The simple thing is that whatever comes under the influence of sexual intercourse, whether it is divine Kundalini or demonic conduct, its effect increases manifold. Sexual intercourse is a most amazing and mysterious activity, on which adequate and unbiased research has not been done due to hesitation and various other social reasons. Well, its secret is well hidden in Tantrashastras. If sexual intercourse is allowed to happen along with Kundalini Yoga done regularly, and if it is done in Tantric method, then it helps the most in the activation and awakening of Kundalini. But if sexual intercourse is done without regular practice of Kundalini Yoga and without

Tantric method, then it can play the most important role in destroying Kundalini.

In fact, hunger for sexual intercourse is also a form of hunger for Kundalini awakening. Any ordinary person resorts to sexual intercourse for such a pleasurable experience in front of which all other pleasurable experiences become pale in comparison. Kundalini awakening is also such a great pleasure, which is much greater than the pleasure of sexual intercourse, but the common man finds sexual intercourse to be the greatest pleasure. There is a lot of similarity between both types of experiences. In reality, sexual pleasure gradually increases and moves towards becoming samadhi-pleasure itself, but most of the time this does not happen. The main reasons for this are, not having sexual intercourse through Tantric method, not maintaining the orgasm for maximum number of days, not having the mental samadhi picture marked, not meditating regularly with Kundalini Yoga, sexual intercourse being considered sexual yoga (sexual intercourse + Kundalini Yoga), and having attachment towards the consort, especially towards her external appearance. Premyogi Vajra used to feel a slight effect of that momentary glimpse of spiritual knowledge even through sexual intercourse. He felt relatively more closeness between the nature of sexual pleasure and the pleasure of Kundalini awakening, although it was natural for there to be a difference in the level of pleasure. After sexual intercourse, he felt the activity of his Kundalini increased. Kundalini awakening seemed to him to be a sophisticated, spiritual/tantric, human and high-power transformation of sexual intercourse. Similarly, he experienced his transformation even after momentary enlightenment, and also after sexual yoga.

With continuous meditation on the invisible/transcendent Kundalini (God, Guru Etc.), the mental power of the seeker remains fully active. This makes Kundalini appear real/physical. When one comes face to face with a real or physical lover in time, then the mental picture of that lover in his mind appears even more real than the physical real one, i.e. super-real. Due to this, despite being untouched by physical attachment (because the habit of holding a mental picture without any physical association has been inculcated in him since before Yoga), a great attraction is created in his mind towards his lover, and his mind becomes fully immersed in that mental image. That is why, right from childhood, one is encouraged to do sadhana and to keep company of seekers, so that in the beginning of adolescence, when there is a surge of energy, and when that seeker comes face to face with a real lover like romantic figure etc., then he/she will become situated in samadhi without any kind of physical contact and fulfil themselves. By this, both the opposite goals are achieved simultaneously, that is, sociality is maintained and one also gets the results of Tantric sadhana. In fact, both yoga practice and sexual intercourse share some similarities spiritually. Yoga practice mostly compensates for the lack of sexual intercourse that is why many yogis are able to remain celibate for life. In reality, people resort to sexual intercourse only to attain a glimpse of Samadhi. However, this deal is very expensive. If one develops the habit of practicing yoga since childhood, then sexual crimes in adolescence can be avoided. If a child engaged in spiritual practice indirectly experiences sexual attraction during his adolescence, his daily spiritual practice suddenly ignites and takes him to enlightenment. As mentioned earlier, exactly the same thing happened with Premyogi Vajra.

Both sexual intercourse and sexual yoga are similar from the external point of view, because both generate excellent mentality with self-awareness, but in ordinary sexual intercourse this mentality/self-awareness is scattered, versatile and extroverted; Whereas in sex yoga, it is concentrated and introverted, giving importance to Kundalini, or it is completely limited to Kundalini only, due to which Kundalini soon gets awakened (rising from the state of dreamlike picture at the time of practice, to the state of awakening). Probably awakening can be experienced more in kundalini form of real person than in physical or gross or non-real forms' images. This also means that all the human things and all the human emotions that generate higher mentality are also helpful in Kundalini awakening. It is worth keeping in mind here that the mentality arising from inhuman sources creates duality with Tamoguna, which harms Kundalini. This means that if a Kundalini Yogi takes shelter of the fruits of his actions filled with humanity and mentality, he quickly attains the benefits of Kundalini. Same thing happened with Premyogi Vajra also. Whatever mentality he acquired from worldly/human activities like service, music, friendship, writing, love, reconciliation, love relationship, sexual relationship etc., he used it to raise the Kundalini through Kundalini Yoga. He was able to do this only when, while performing the above mentioned worldly activities, he kept his Kundalini alive by adopting the non-duality adopted by the body-man. On the contrary, if a person maintains a high mentality without keeping the Kundalini alive in his mind, then it seems natural that this does not strengthen the Kundalini, but only increases self-delusion. It seems that in order to keep this mental Kundalini alive, special emphasis has been given in all religions on regular spiritual practice. Sadhana can also be personal. For example, for a long time Premyogi Vajra did not get time to do separate religious sadhana, but the Shavid he was building became his sadhana, because due to the influence of his Dvaitadvaita arising of it, his Kundalini was in his mind almost continuously existing. This proves that just as by strengthening Advaita, Kundalini itself gets strengthened, similarly by strengthening Kundalini, Advaita itself gets strengthened. There is a Kundalini residing in the mind of every person, because everyone needs a reliable and strong source of mental happiness, which can be useful in times of material poverty or during attachment to duality, but very few people give importance to that Kundalini of theirs. Probably the same Kundalini provides shelter to a person in various types of physical helplessness, such as old age, illness, weakness, social exclusion etc. The same Kundalini supports the person after death, until he gets a fixed physical body or salvation.

Kundalini theory also works behind Shavid and Vedas and Puranas, because while worshiping the humanoid beings and gods mentioned in them, the Kundalini of the mind gets imposed on them (because the transcendental gods automatically get the form of transcendental/mental Kundalini), and she becomes confirmed. It is written at most places in Hindu philosophy that do not get misled by the senses, do not get carried away by attachment, make sacrifices, behave with simplicity etc.; all that points towards Kundalini awakening. In fact, after Kundalini awakening, all the qualities mentioned above arise automatically. Similarly, God or Guru is considered the basis of life because it is he who develops in the mind and becomes Kundalini, which is the best basis of life. It has also been proved in the Shavid book that Kundalini is the basis of exercise, action and sexuality. Life is actually made up of exercise, action and sex. In fact, keeping the Kundalini in the form of a Guru or a God in the mind is acceptable in the polite society, not keeping the Kundalini in the form of a sexual lover. Wearing the Kundalini of a sexual lover is considered in the category of adultery.

Actually, Premyogi Vajra had a relationship with the physical form of his second Kundalini right from his birth, and with the help of Shavid, that mental picture of Kundalini kept flashing in his mind from time to time for about the above mentioned 20 years. At the beginning of Shavidnirman, once Premyogi Vajra had narrowly escaped from sexual crime due to the divine mercy of God, because at that time even a little influence of enlightenment was left in him. At that time, he did not have any knowledge of both Kundalini Yoga and sexual Yoga, yet due to unknown motivation, he had indirectly (unknowingly) come under the influence of Jaunasansarga or sexual Yoga. Therefore, in ordinary cases, this yoga can be free from side effects only under the guidance of a qualified guru and proper method. Its knowledge should be given only to an intensely curious and deserving person. One should not even joke about sexual yoga with people who are ignorant of it, because they can interpret it in the opposite way and misuse this knowledge. Most of the people have the misconception that Tantric sex yoga has side effects on worldly activities. They get this confusion because they start comparing sex yoga with ordinary sex. In fact, there is a world of difference between these two. They also start comparing a sex yogi with an ordinary sannyasi yogi, because both of them look similar from outside, although from within, tantra yogis are all-rounders. In fact, sexual yoga is a tremendous energy. This energy helps immensely in the progress of both spiritual and material fields. It seems to be true that complete sexual satisfaction is possible only through sexual yoga. It is this lack of satisfaction that, in most cases, leads to bitterness in married life. Premyogi Vajra also felt that this type of bitterness had diminished through this yoga.

It appears that the power embedded in the tantra itself became the cause of the tantra's own social collapse. Tantric had the divine radiance of Kundalini and self-knowledge, due to which most of the things they said and thought from their heart were proved to be true. That is why mischievous people were afraid of them. They could not confront the Tantric directly, that is why by hatching a conspiracy, Tantric and Tantric Vidya were discredited and almost ostracized in most of the societies. Tantricas have a sense of non-duality, due to which their mental power remains protected from getting wasted. Due to the intensity of that accumulated mental power, their vision is very sharp and effective. That vision burns away the evil of bad people, which people who are bad by nature are unable to tolerate because of their false ego. That's why instead of blaming themselves, they start blaming the Tantric.

Kundalini Yoga is like a mechanical machine that produces enlightenment. Therefore, man has to carefully preserve his human qualities (self-knowledge causing natural factors) like love etc., because under the influence of Kundalini Yoga, he can ignore human emotions. However, Kundalini Yoga with human emotions is more effective. Nowadays, Kundalini Yoga can be practiced easily with the help of internet, e-book reader and education websites like Quora, because all the knowledge nowadays previously given in esoteric form has become free from such bondage.

Some fatigue is also present due to sexual yoga. For this reason, the feeling/glimpse of Kundalini awakening probably cannot be endured for more than a few moments. To experience full awakening, maintaining full body-mind functionality requires a balanced life and a balanced diet, possibly including some quality non-vegetarian food. With all such Panchamkaras, that lifestyle becomes almost a complete Tantric way of life. Although this method is difficult, and possibly without a qualified master, it can have serious consequences. The method of complete awakening and without danger seems to be the simple Kundalini Yoga method, practiced only by Sanyasi Yogis. But for immediate success in this, one has to sacrifice the world. Although some sacrifice has to be made for the success of sexual yoga also. Similarly, through sex yoga, one can experience a glimpse of enlightenment, perhaps only for a few moments, as Premyogi Vajra did. Probably, complete knowledge of self can be attained only through combined efforts of renunciation and spiritual practice. After the momentary enlightenment, some divine inspirational force was constantly pushing Premyogi Vajra towards Sannyasayoga, but ultimately he ignored it, succumbing to the resistance of the world. Seeing no way out, he had to adopt the worldly path, albeit with a Tantric way of life. It can also be called the path of Karmayoga or the middle path of Buddhists. Inspired by the success of this path, he created the philosophy of physiology.

For spiritual practice, virtual renunciation also works. For example, when Premyogi Vajra felt a bit lonely, he maintained a connection with people from other corners of the earth and discussed Kundalini Yoga on the internet. From this he also got the fruits of virtual renunciation, and his knowledge related to Kundalini Yoga also increased. Due to this, he was engaged in worldly activities like renunciation, because incomplete contact with incomplete acquaintances on the internet gives results like renunciation. In addition, night and day were also joined with it, which is the main sign of knowledge. In fact, when it is day in one corner of the earth, it is night in the other corner.

Kundalini awakening leads to self-knowledge only indirectly. The only and direct reason for self-knowledge is concentration meditation. Even if concentration meditation continues for a long time without Kundalini awakening, through yoga practice etc. or due to sexual attraction or for any other reason, then enlightenment is still possible, as happened with Premyogi Vajra at the time of indirect Tantra. Kundalini awakening only helps in maintaining focused attention, because the multi-million dollar Kundalini experienced at the time of awakening keeps attracting the person towards itself again and again. If even after Kundalini awakening, concentration cannot be maintained continuously, then that Kundalini awakening does not seem to have any special significance. That is why perhaps after experiencing Kundalini awakening, the Yogi is advised to live a calm, stress-free, greed-free, rational and non-dual life, so that he can continuously concentrate on Kundalini. In various religions, especially in Sanatan Dharma, the importance of concentration is described everywhere. Advaita is also strengthened through this concentrated meditation, which is essential for liberation.

At the time of Kundalini awakening, the entire brain focuses all its energy on a single mental picture (Kundalini). With this the picture becomes alive and visible. There seems to be no reason not to believe that modern neuro-science cannot produce such a condition artificially. Today science has advanced a lot. Similarly, according to Premyogi Vajra, if enlightenment arises from a picture that resides continuously in the mind, then perhaps that picture can be maintained even with the help of modern psychological instruments. Some people believe that instead of concentrated meditation in the form of yoga, one should practice Sakshikarana means witnessing (toward resolutions). In fact, Kundalini awakening occurs only through concentrated meditation. Although self-knowledge can be attained through Sakshikarana or even directly, but Kundalini awakening is the fastest, most natural, most scientific, most practical, simplest and most reliable method of self-knowledge.

Interest and disinterest are a different matter, and truth is a different matter. Any subject can be called distasteful, but its truth cannot be denied. For example, spirituality may be distasteful to most people, but its authenticity cannot be doubted. By continuously accepting the truth, gradually even disinterest gets transformed into interest. Mahatma Buddha has also said that there are ups and downs in life, but the truth should always be accepted. How can those who do not accept the authenticity of the truth end their disinterest in the truth? Those who accept the truth, the truth itself keeps moving towards them.

A question arises in the minds of many people whether Kundalini Yoga should be done with the eyes open or closed. In fact, the main and only aim of Yoga should be to develop Kundalini, no matter what human method one has to resort to for this. Kundalini is a mental picture, which does not require eyes to see. Only external images are visible to the eyes. External images can interfere with the contemplation of the internal image. By the way, when Kundalini awakening is taking place, at that time open eyes cannot create disturbance in the mental picture, because at that time most of the energy of the brain is being used in awakening Kundalini, due to which Kundalini is at the level of maximum expression. Eyes also work like a camera. To capture an image outside, the camera's shutter opens, and then closes, so that the image can be developed inside the camera. Similarly, we keep our eyes open to capture our favourite physical picture correctly and in detail, and during yoga, we keep our eyes closed to fix it in our mind.

In reality, mantra is just a tact to provide life to Kundalini. While reciting the mantra, the prana that is emitted through the mouth keeps on strengthening the Kundalini which is situated/imagined at the idol, Sun, any other place or unknown place etc. That is why there should be only one Ishta

Mantra, because by repeated memorization it becomes fully memorized, due to which there is no need to use any force in the brain to speak it. Due to this, brain power is left to strengthen the Kundalini. If Kundalini is meditated at the beginning of mantra chanting, then Kundalini automatically keeps getting its power during the entire chanting. In a way, Kundalini gets associated with that mantra. This is the success of mantra, and this is also the secret of chanting. Similarly, if Kundalini is meditated at the beginning of listening to music, then the entire music keeps strengthening the Kundalini. Perhaps this is the hidden secret behind remembering the presiding deity (Kundalini) while starting all the works. Similarly, Prana also comes out through breath and keeps strengthening the Kundalini. Kundalini should be meditated on the Vishuddhichakra, at the place where the sound is generated. There one can also meditate on the sound of Om etc. This also gives strength to speech. Prana keeps igniting the Kundalini, and Kundalini keeps drawing Prana (life air). In this way, Prana and Kundalini, at one place (at the place of Kundalini), continuously enhance each other. Meditation is like using giving air to an ember, first a spark of fire is created in it, then air is continued to be given, due to which that spark gets converted into a flame of fire, of course then there is no need of continuous attention towards it to keep it burning. In the same way, if by generating the spark of Kundalini, if continuous attention is given to the falling of vital air on it, then it itself becomes clear and fierce like the flame of fire, even if there is no continuous direct attention kept on it subsequently. Although it should be kept in mind that kundalini is present at that particular chakra/place, and the Kundalini flame is flaring with Pranavayu. It can also be understood in this way that if there is difficulty in meditating Kundalini on any chakra, then one should meditate on the falling breath on the chakra. Due to this, with the power of life, the Kundalini picture starts emerging there spontaneously. While putting the breath on the Kundalini located on the chakra, if after some time the Kundalini starts appearing at another place, then it should be considered as the flare-up of the Kundalini fire that has much flared up and has run away and should be allowed to flare up at its desired place. After some time, it shrinks to that chakra itself, or moves to another chakra. Similarly, Kundalini's colourful facial features, her colourful physical conditions and her colourful actions should be understood as like the colourful flames of

Agni. Whichever Chakra the Kundalini is on, it should be understood that due to the pull and pressure of the Bandhas, the energy of the entire body is gathering there. Due to this the Kundalini itself gets agitated. In reality, body, mind and everything else is also a form of life or vital air or prana, nothing else. In Yoga, everything is available only through Prana (subtle and meditative vital air). Kundalini rises above the Muladhar only with the help of life force. When Kundalini passes from one chakra to another, it passes in the form of prana. There is great power in life. When the pressure of Moolabandha is released by exhaling and holding it there, then the Kundalini falls on its own along with the life force on to the lower chakra. First of all, by inhaling the breath, it is poured over the Kundalini located above the chakra, and that breath is captured there by applying Jalandhar Bandha. When the Kundalini becomes clear there, and the Prana starts trying to descend from there, then it is lifted up again with the Moolabandha and is raised up to the Kundalini. Due to this, pressure of prana is created on the Kundalini from both the top and bottom, and it becomes clearly active on that chakra. While doing yoga, especially asanas and pranayama, it is easier to ignite the Kundalini at the base. Many times, especially when the mind is too agitated, initially the Kundalini has to be fixed with a little force through the mind at the Mooladhara Chakra. Then it itself starts getting strengthened with life. For this, as soon as the breath (Prana) goes in, one has to experience a rustling or movement or a shock or only meditation in the Muladhar area and sometimes also in the Swadhisthana area. A slight rustle or a slight shock means that the prana has hit the Kundalini. This makes the Kundalini shine especially. According to the same principle, in the main part of Kundalini Yoga, Kundalini rotation, after holding the breath on a chakra, and after meditating on the Kundalini there, taking normal breath as per the need, return the breath to that chakra. Feel it falling there and the Kundalini getting ignited by it. When the breathing becomes very weak, and it seems that the breath has filled the stomach, it means the chakra has satisfied, then repeat the same process on the lower chakra. When Kundalini is meditated on Swadhisthana and Muladhar Chakras; then while exhaling, a slight upward contraction of the muscle should be made at the Muladharachakrabindu, and for meditating the Swadhisthanachakrabindu, the Muladharachakra should be slightly pushed upwards with the help of

Muladhara muscle, so that the prana (Apana) below also reaches the Swadhisthanachakra. Such pressure can be maintained continuously, even when the breath is falling on them. By the above efforts, the breath/prana is accurately aimed at the Muladhar-Kundalini, and at the Swadhisthana-Kundalini, Prana and Apana get together and mix, due to which the Kundalini starts glowing on the respective chakras. After Kapalbhati Pranayama, by applying all the Bandhas, when an attempt is made to raise the Kundalini above the Muladhar, then by concentrating on the Muladhar Chakra, it gets slightly compressed. Due to this, Kundalini gets collected from the surrounding area and gets deposited on that subtle chakra point. She then rises up through the Uddiyana Bandha. By applying Jalandhar Bandha at that time, especially during the practice period of a new yogi, there may be some difficulty in reaching the Kundalini to the brain, because the neck remains bent in it. Therefore, Jalandhar Bandha cannot be imposed. On the Muladhar Chakra, its slight contraction keeps the Kundalini glowing, and with help of Uddiyana Bandha means flying lock, there is an upward pull on it. As it moves towards the brain, the Muladhara (Moolabandha) should be left loose, so that there is no downward pull on the Kundalini, and it can easily go up, like an arrow released from the bow. Muladhar Chakra is like a fire pit, in which Kundalini gets ignited with vital air. Probably that is why it is called Kundalini (Kund + Lini, consciousness sleeping in the pit). The Muladhara Chakra is also located at the bottom of the body, in the centre of the line connecting the genitals to the anus, and also in the back of the body, at the lowest point of the spine. As per requirement, Kundalini meditation can be done at either of the two places. While doing Yogasana etc. and during practical activities, it seems easier to meditate in the back part, especially those which involve bend in the waist, and in the front part while doing Pranayama in Siddhasana etc. By the way, after practice, the Muladhara with the spine starts to appear superior. By the way, the base of the back appears to be very powerful. There the Kundalini fire seems to be burning with the most clarity, and from there its upward movement also seems to be most clear. Premyogi Vajra did not need this method of measuring the position of the chakras by measuring it with a tape. He only made an approximate assessment. It may be possible that accurate determination of the chakras is required only in the higher stages of yoga.

Vedas, Puranas, God's hymns and kirtans etc. have been created so that Dvaitadvaita can become more established and strengthened during their practice, because sometimes due to excessive busyness during worldly activities, Dvaitadvaita does not get proper prestige. Similarly, in the peaceful period after busyness, if duality is extinguished with help of shavid, then all the old fatigue of body and mind disappears, and the person gets up to do new work with double the enthusiasm. The karmic bondages created by doing deeds also get weakened by this. Modern scientists also say that actions and resolutions etc. do not become complete just by doing the work, because they remain present in the mind in seed form. It is only through Yoga/contemplation related to the Karma done after the Karma that the Karma becomes fully performed. In fact, through yoga/peaceful contemplation, those actions/resolutions re-appear in the mind, towards which detachment is present on its own, although detachment remains present to a greater extent due to the practice of awareness under the influence of yoga. This calms them down.

In today's dense population times, tantric sex is the best way to control population. This has brought happiness in marriage, spiritual development and fearlessness from an unwanted pregnancy, three in one.

Both Shavid and Kundalini Yoga work together. When attention is focused on Kundalini, then Shavid is achieved through Kundalini Yoga. When there is a state of mental oscillation, then the help of Shavid's Advaita is taken. Advaita of Shavid stops or pacifies the useless/harmful types of emotions and sensations, and creates a positive environment in the brain. This conserves mental energy, which automatically strengthens the Kundalini. However, ultimately both the methods strengthen the Kundalini. In sex yoga, the separate personality of the consort is not seen. In this, two bodies as subtle countries are seen forming a relationship, their body-beings are seen, and their two kings are seen, or a king and a queen are seen. The concept of Shavid is constantly kept in mind. Each part of the body is experienced according to Shavid, This itself keeps the pure mental Kundalini image strengthened, because Kundalini is actually a form given to the subtly physical body-man. In reality the Kundalini which is meditated upon; it is mostly in the form of a non-dual guru, a deity or some other loving person. The Kundalini in the form of a deity or a deceased person is even more non-dual, because the feelings of both life and death are simultaneously present in it.

There is one more mysterious thing. The way a person himself becomes proficient in Tantric sex yoga by living a life full of meditation, non-duality, non-attachment, peaceful, free from mental disorders and blissful; in the same way, the above mentioned qualities automatically arise from mental Nityasamadhi (through Tantric sexual yoga) in someone's form, especially in the form of a goddess. This is also the secret of Kundalini Yoga/Tantric Sexual Yoga. Same thing happened with Premyogi Vajra. Because the Nityasamadhi of the form of the first goddess had automatically entered his mind due to sexual attraction, hence all the above mentioned qualities automatically arose in him, which took him to the aforesaid momentary self-knowledge.

Guru had become firmly attached to the mind of Premyogi Vajra since the time the first goddess had joined his mind. The pictures of both of them lived together in his mind. Those two pictures kept enhancing each other. Even before his marriage, with the help of the one verse Tantrashastra written by him as mentioned above in the book, the picture of Guru had been established in his mind without any marital relations, even before marriage. The same picture encouraged him to get married as soon as possible, because he wanted the Kundalini picture to awaken. Due to the same loyal belief of the mind, his married life automatically, without his knowledge, got converted into Tantra, and he kept activating the Kundalini. Although, contrary to expectations, her early married life was not as sweet. Many a times, due to the stress arising from his busy and competitive worldly life, he would even get into a minor scuffle with his wife. Then how suddenly such a big change took place in him that he was able to generate the harmony of sexual yoga. In fact, this was possible only due to the power of Kundalini burning in him due to his non-duality, especially with help of Shavid. People close to him and other acquaintances; especially those who considered themselves pure or virtuous, spiritual, religious, idealistic and public teacher etc. with attachment and ego; they kept dealing with him indirectly or less openly or rather in a hidden manner, probably because of his Tantric approach. The author observed at one place that at the time of marriage, there was a tradition of making the bride sit directly on the lap of a Brahmin priest (guru) and giving her blessings by that guru. In fact, due to this, the picture of the Guru gets linked with the picture of the bride, thereby increasing the chances of the groom getting the benefit of indirect tantra. This means that practice was based on Tantra. This proves that most of the beliefs and practices of the Hindu system are psychological or tantric.

All living beings feel a special attachment to the one, whose Kundalini is active. There is an atmosphere of happiness and stresslessness around him. The people around him look at him with love and respect. They become as cool, nondual and loving as him. Premyogi Vajra had all these experiences, and even on the day of awakening he had a small feeling of devotion towards himself. Near Kundalini awakening, a person finds favourable conditions all around. No one can harm him even if anyone wants to. On the contrary, the evil thrown towards him is transformed into his good. His suppressed wishes also start getting fulfilled, it is not surprising, because Kundalini understands everything. In fact, Kundalini itself gives a personality to a person. Most of the people are living life without personality.

While practicing active Advaita like Shavid, there comes a time when the person becomes transformed. His mind starts to remain blank, his memory power decreases, and he starts to remain isolated from everyone. His ability to think and take decisions also decreases. That stage is only the beginning stage of his Kundalini awakening stage. Feeling somewhat disturbed and doubtful by this, he himself turns towards Kundalini Yoga. This transformation does not mean that any physical structure of his brain changes, but rather that his nature and outlook are transformed. He becomes non-dual, unattached, full of sattva qualities, blissful and loving to all living beings. It is possible that the subtle neuronal circuits of his brain get upgraded, because those neural circuits determine the behaviour and outlook of the person. For this, along with a calm, comfortable, loving, spiritual and cooperative environment, other favourable conditions should also be available; exactly what is needed for the development of a child. If a favourable environment is not found, the transformation becomes very slow, and may even stop until the above mentioned cordial and spiritual environment is available. Because Premyogi Vajra had got all the above mentioned suitable conditions almost on time, hence his transformation got a strong push due to which his Kundalini was awakened. Such transformation should continue even after Kundalini awakening, until enlightenment. Although then we can make do with fewer adaptations than before. Even after enlightenment, minor favours should be received and sadhana should be continued, otherwise his transformation may also be reversed, due to which the yogi may again reach back to normal state, because everything is relative. After Kundalini awakening, because the transformation is happening at a fast pace, which requires more energy, the speed of breathing also increases. Mental transformation also leads to physical transformation, such as increased blood flow to the brain and improvement in brain function, etc., so that the samadhi image can persist. When Premyogi Vajra started transforming after Kundalini awakening, the same symptoms started repeating in him, which had arisen during his tantric samadhi before his momentary spiritual knowledge. In his mind, by overpowering the Kundalini of the form of the first goddess, the Kundalini of that old spiritual man was getting strengthened, which was consuming a large part of the body's energy. He was beginning to feel tired. His mind became filled with great joy and became calm. The brain circuits of the old Kundalini and its related matters were diminishing, and new nerve circuits related to the new Kundalini were being formed. He was continuing to develop like a child, and he was also sleeping well. The perception power of his brain was increasing etc. Because he had experienced his Kundalini (mental elder spiritual man) as his soul, hence such new nerve circuits were being formed in his brain, which could always keep the picture of his Guru in his mind. The common man does not have such special circuits due to which he experiences darkness as his soul. The reason for this is that they do not have that Samadhi (Kundalini awakening) which connects the bright picture of the Guru/Kundalini with the dark soul that is wandering since time immemorial. Same Samadhi upgrades/updates the brain. Also, in the Samadhi/Kundalini awakening, the dark soul becomes one with the shining Kundalini, that is, the soul becomes light. Due to this, the seeker, unknowingly, himself gets engaged in the campaign of purifying his soul. Because the soul can be purified only through non-duality, hence non-duality itself starts developing in him, which also positively transforms his lifestyle.

The secret of the religious war is also hidden in the scripture itself. In fact, practicing Advaita in problematic situations is of great benefit. What could be a bigger problem than death? But in reality there should be only fear of death, not actual death. What kind of knowledge, what kind of Kundalini awakening and what kind of liberation does anyone get after death? That is why in the religious scriptures, there are descriptions of war and death at various places, so that the fear of death remains. Perhaps in the original form of some extremist religions, such a symbolic religious war was alluded to, but later it was misinterpreted or mischaracterized by inexperienced scholars. Similarly, if Advaita is adopted even in happy/emotional moments, then the Kundalini strengthened by it provides support even in sorrow/absence. It has also been said that everyone should remember in happiness, but no one do it; if one remembers in happiness then why should there be sorrow?

While doing Yogasana and Pranayama, each inward breath (Prana) should be felt as falling on the Kundalini picture. Due to this, the Kundalini picture remains continuous and its clarity also increases; no matter on which chakra it is placed, even if it is not on any chakra and is placed anywhere, such as in any part of the body, sky, unknown place etc. Life force can be provided to Kundalini by the movement of breath on both sides. For example, if the Kundalini is at the navel chakra, then it is given life force from the upper side, through the inward breath, and from the lower side, through the outward breath. In this way, wherever the Kundalini is, it can be strengthened by both inhalation and exhalation. Kundalini fire can be ignited by both the in and out breaths simultaneously, especially at the time of Kapalbhati; like a hand fan, the fire gets strengthened by the winds from both the directions. At the time of Kapalbhati, you can also meditate on the breath giving power to the Kundalini on the Muladhar, just as air gives power to an engine. Just like the smoke of an engine comes out, similarly the waste air of Kundalini i.e. its smoke can be felt coming out. Imagine the breath going in, falling on the Kundalini, and keep that kundalini thought in your mind, then leave the mind loose, so that it can move freely. Whatever one thinks along with that kundalini thought, through the power of all these thoughts the Kundalini gets strengthened. There should be less coercion with the mind. It should be controlled with love, tact and without harming one's freedom. Reflecting these facts, it is said in the scriptures that by controlling the life force, the mind is controlled, that is, the mind can be controlled only through the life force, not otherwise. The life force that comes out from the sound of music should also be felt in the form of energy falling on the Kundalini, no matter where the Kundalini is experienced. This is also a type of Sangeet Yoga, which is very effective. Music also indirectly strengthens Kundalini. In fact, Advaita is strengthened through songs. Through new and old songs, the life experienced in old and new times is again remembered. By imposing non-duality on the feelings arising from it, Advaita gets immense confirmation, due to which Kundalini also gets strengthened. In Chakrasadhana (kundalini rotation), while holding the breath by applying yogic bandha, one should feel the gathering of air (prana) of the whole body on each chakra one by one as mentioned above and the fire of the Kundalini picture is ignited through it. Just as the physical flower blooms due to the upward rise of the earth's power and the downward passage of the sun's power and both meeting together; in the same way, along with the in breath (Pran) which is filled from top to bottom, the Prana going down and pushed further with help of Jalandhara Bandha as applied as per the need, and the Apana means lower Prana rising up with help of Moola Bandha and Uddiyana Bandha, meet at a place or especially on the Kundalini Chakra, means both come together and get mixed; with that he mental flower (Kundalini) blooms there.

By the way, Premyogi Vajra, during the 20 years of Shavid's practice, was also in the company of Sanatan Dharma and culture or people who practice them. What this means is that if along with the influence of Shavid, the influence of Sanatan Dharma-Culture also continues to fall on the psyche, then the spiritual goal is achieved very quickly.

When the Kundalini is on the Muladhar Chakra, while holding the breath, when Uddiyana Bandha and Moola Bandha are engaged, an imaginary sucking type column is created by them to the brain. That pillar keeps pulling the Kundalini upwards. Additionally, Moolabandha also pushes the Kundalini upwards. Due to this, the Kundalini gradually rises upwards and reaches the brain. In this way, there are two forces acting together, the pull-force of Uddiyanabandha and the push-force of Mulabandha.

A lot of emphasis has been laid on Titiksha in the scriptures. This means that one should tolerate all emotions while remaining detached and non-dual. But there is little description of the ways to tolerate them. Shavid is also a major and very effective way to cope with them. In reality, emotions are not bad, because they remain present even in a liberated body. The evil lies in the feeling of being badly influenced by them, which is not there in the body-man. For example, there is no harm in feeling joy and sadness, because these are natural and human qualities of consciousness. By meditating on the body having body-men, this type of illusion of seeing truthfulness in those emotions gets destroyed immediately, and the person becomes free from their influence. There is no problem in being influenced a little, but a worrying situation occurs when due to their influence, the person goes out of his control, a pang like feeling dominates inside him, and his mental peace is affected. Along with this his mental happiness also gets disturbed. Like the body man, one can pretend to be influenced by the body and mind, but one should never mistake it for truth. Similarly, there seems to be no harm in experiencing mental defects, if one remains unaffected by them.

Many times the effect of a person's conduct is not even visible, but it definitely has an impact, which gradually accumulates and over time leads to spiritual transformation. The effect of Shavid also depends on the company around, also depends on the type of livelihood and deeds, also depends on the speed of actions and emotions, also depends on health and age, and also on loyalty/dedication towards Shavid. Moreover, also depends on the quantity and quality of meditation on it.

Premyogi Vajra felt that people had more faith in the Vishamvahi or direct tantra than the Samavahi or indirect tantra. They looked at the Samvahi tantra with inferiority. They felt that keeping a woman in one's mind was against manliness. Due to the fear of this inferiority, Premyogi Vajra never tried to awaken the Kundalini of the first Devi Rani, although the momentary knowledge of the soul, which is said to be the result of Kundalini awakening, was achieved by the daily natural mental samadhi of the form of Devi Rani, without Kundalini awakening. In fact, Kundalini awakening also gives rise to this type of Nityasamadhi. Another reason for that thinking of the people could also be that perhaps most of the people did not have such girlfriends or wives who had these three qualities of desire, attractiveness and strong self-control together, towards whom unlimited attraction would arise in the mind. In any case, cohabitation with a religious wife is difficult, because by living with her every day and with the firm belief that she will always be with him, the attraction towards her decreases rather than increases. Probably he also felt with misunderstanding that direct samadhi-relation could be made only through indirect sexual relationship (samavahi) of Apratyakshatantra, which he considered anti-social, especially before marriage; and not through the direct sexual tantra/sexual relations of indirect tantra. However, as mentioned above, his misunderstanding proved to be fruitful as it proved that maximum attraction can be generated through symbolic sex of indirect tantra, which is in the form of samadhi, and there is no anti-sociality in it. Probably, in order to avoid inferiority/humiliation related to his own family, his mind had, unknowingly, completely rejected the existence of Pratyaksha Tantra. Because he did not have knowledge of the vishamavahi tantra of the Pratyakshatantra category, he seemed to be experiencing inferiority related to his love affair. In contrast, majority of the married people did not have knowledge of the symbolic means pure mental form tantra of indirect tantra category, hence they stayed away from it. Premyogi Vajra had received quick and powerful Kundalini benefits by the mixture of both Samavahi and Vishamavahi Tantra (both in balanced form in a tactical way to be saved from anti-sociality while reaping benefits of both) of Apratyaksha Tantra with the first Devi Queen.

Some people say that non-dualism or witnessing is the best practice, while others say that concentration or contemplation is the best. In fact, a combination of both is best. If you cannot combine both, then you should do Ekagrata means concentration Sadhana in the form of Kundalini Yoga for at least 1 hour each in the morning and evening, and throughout the day, you should do Advaita Sadhana or Sakshikarana Sadhana like the body-man, which is also called Karma Yoga. Gyan Yoga in the morning and evening and Karma Yoga throughout the day. In fact, both the methods strengthen the Kundalini, and both also strengthen Advaita/Sakshibhava. If Advaita Bhava can strengthen Kundalini, then why can't Kundalini strengthen Advaita? The glory of Advaita is great. Spiritual development through Advaita happens automatically, there is no need to do anything special. One keeps getting inspiration to move forward on one's own. If Advaita is continuously maintained, then no one can stop the enlightenment. Witnessing and Advaita are the same thing. Through witnessing also, like Advaita, it is proved that everything is equal, because in this nothing is weighed (JUDGE) or tested, but an equal detached feeling towards everything is maintained, due to which Advaita itself is proved. Therefore, witnessing also strengthens the Kundalini.

Premyogi Vajra used to treat everyone in his class equally. Different types of students studied in his class. Some were white, some were black and some were golden; some were attractive, some were ordinary; some were tall, some were short. Although his behaviour with everyone was non-dual like, polite, friendly, practical, progressive, humanitarian, cheerful and full of hard work, just like the body-man of the body-society. The similar was others' towards him. Really a good community that was. An excellent teacher had lovingly named him Chameleon because he used to blend in completely with everyone without abandoning Advaita. This was possible only with the company of that old spiritual man. What could be a better example of Advaita than that? In the same way, there were different types of people living in his house and in the surrounding society, who also lived together in the same way. Probably at that time Advaita was strongly established in the society as a result of people's reverence for the Puranas. He did not like non-dual and non-vegetarian people, although he did not feel hatred, but love and attachment towards non-dual and loving type of partial non-vegetarians, and they too towards Premyogi Vajra, especially after he attained enlightenment. This proves that probably Advaita and nonveg and alcohol may be keeping reinforcing each other, if there is Tantric belief. The true eternal principle of karma-fruit relationship remains the same, only the perspective improves. This principle is tantra-valid too. Although the guidance of a Sadhguru is essential in this, otherwise the nature of the practitioner may get distorted. In fact, there is no harm in having a good knowledge of differences, but there is only harm in creating a feeling of inferiority in someone through a dualistic view. Everyone's contribution is equally expected for a healthy society. Kundalini awakening is more accessible to the humanist and idealistic Golden Society, because it is easier to meditate on a person or Guru who is in the form of a charming person and side by side heavily indulged in spiritual practice. That's why only a special person from the so called upper Varna was made the Guru. But for self-knowledge, it also has to depend on other Varna-communities, because without a society of mixed varnas and gunas, the perfection of Advaita cannot be achieved. With that non-duality, one gets rid of the attachment to the physical form of the shining Kundalini, which is essential for enlightenment, because through it, the mental Kundalini quickly becomes strong and mature, and then falls like a ripe fruit, into the infinite ocean of enlightenment. Because Advaita also strengthens Kundalini, and the non-dual feeling held within a community of people of different Varnas and qualities is very strong, hence it is also proved that dark skinned people also have an important contribution in the awakening of Kundalini. Similarly, mostly people of lower Varna have to depend on the upper Varna as gurus/priests/gods etc. for Kundalini awakening. However, to become a guru, a person of the golden category must have high standards of conduct, spiritual/nondual, self-study; must be virtuous, disciplined, yogi, practical and Vedic-mythological; just like Premyogi vajra's grandfather was. There does not seem to be any other special and immediate benefit just by being identified with the golden category. Therefore, we can see that only through mutual cooperation between different communities, a healthy society is formed and it remains development oriented. Therefore, diversity should be preserved. If an attempt is made to destroy the differences due to inter-community closeness, then the unique benefits derived from those differences also start getting destroyed. An attempt has been made to explain the same principle through the churning of the ocean described in the Puranas. The sea is the symbol of the world there. The various resources that emerged from the sea are symbols of material comforts. The nectar that comes out along with it is a symbol of salvation. The gods there appear symbols of people who are light skinned, relaxed or Sattvik in their work, clever, powerless and engaged in spiritual practices; and the demons are of dark skinned, strong, simple and hardworking people. When the gods kept failing in the churning of the ocean despite repeated attempts, they had to take the help of demons. It was only through the combined efforts of both the categories that both the goals of material comforts and salvation were simultaneously achieved.

Nothing is achieved in life without paying a price; even the achievements considered spiritual like Kundalini awakening, enlightenment and liberation etc. Premyogi Vajra practiced Shavid continuously for 20 years, and maintained the duality or advaita arising from it, only then he experienced momentary Kundalini awakening. Kundalini Yoga and Sexual Yoga only provided a little extra strength to Kundalini as required for awakening, but it remained active continuously for last 20 years due to the influence of functional Advaita.

Premyogi Vajra had attained perfection. Still, I don't know why he was testing the first goddess? He wanted Devirani to completely surrender herself to him, leaving aside all other concerns, and willingly take the initiative to spend her life with him. Perhaps he had developed a little arrogance due to his incomplete self-knowledge, because "the half-filled pitcher screams more". He also had doubts about the Tantric approach of the Goddess. He wanted to see her completely loyal, loving and detached like Purna-devi. He wants to keep his master happy with her behaviour; he also wanted to make her do true service to him like an auspicious goddess and follow his good orders. He wanted to see her as crazy in his love as Meera or Radha were in Krishna's love. Perhaps she might have been so crazy at heart, but she might not have been able to show her madness due to the fear of public shame. He wanted to see her crazy in love in a Tantric way and also free from the fear of public shame. It is possible that Devi Rani is also keeping all these expectations from Premyogi Vajra. In the mind of Premyogi Vajra, the eternally blissful samadhi of his form was already there, hence why would he sacrifice his samadhi by taking physical initiative. On the contrary, he hoped that through that samadhi he would get another glimpse of enlightenment. It is also possible that the same thing might have happened with Devirani too, that is why she too could not take the initiative. With this, Osho ji's statement once again becomes literally true that in reality sexual intercourse is done only to attain the state of Samadhi.

Taking naps during the day, intermittently, is also a spiritual symptom. This happens due to the fatigue of the non-dual and Kundalini mind. It is not a bad thing to get carried away by emotions and sensations, but they should be controlled quickly by meditation of the non-dual Shavid present in one's own body, otherwise they will cause more harm to the body and mind than benefit.

Perhaps Kundalini awakening has the same effect as daily Kundalini yoga practice. From both, Kundalini constantly settles in the mind. Perhaps even after awakening, one must practice Kundalini Yoga, so that the Kundalini, in the form of Samadhi, can remain steady in the brain, and not fall down. This meant that without Kundalini awakening, self-knowledge or liberation is possible even by regularly practicing Kundalini Yoga. Kundalini awakening however gives additional stability to the Kundalini in addition to yoga practice. Kundalini-samadhi is matured only by regular and continuous yoga practice. Kundalini awakening only gives it an extra strength. However, samadhi produced by sexual attraction does not require yoga and Kundalini awakening, as it is naturally intense. Similarly, as mentioned earlier, when the Kundalini of sexual yoga, which is considered powerful, also replaces the irrational/exciting thoughts that arise during sexual intercourse, then the morning-evening Kundalini yoga practice will surely neutralise the thoughts of relatively low power arising throughout the day. In fact, Kundalini Yoga expends the excess power of the mind in meditating on the Kundalini, so that vain thoughts cannot gain mental power, and eventually they fade away.

As soon as the mental states calm down, darkness prevails in the mind of the enlightened person too, like other ordinary people. Premyogi Vajra was surprised to experience such a thing, and wondered what would be the benefit of attaining enlightenment then? He did not even think that after his death he would start shining. At that time, if anyone asked any mysterious question related to it as generally expected, he would say that he did not know. He naturally lived in a state of non-duality. This means that he gave equal importance to light and darkness. This proves again that one should remain situated in Advaita only, nothing else is special. But it was definitely true that the fear of death had reduced a lot in him, as is the case in an inveterate drug addict.

Many people think that yoga practice does not consume energy. But in reality, it also consumes energy, although much less than the physical and mental labour of daily life. No work is accomplished without power, just out of thin air. Although it is a different matter that through yoga practice, a person learns the proper method of working and behaving; due to which, unnecessary expenditure of energy caused by wrong attitude like lust, anger etc. mental defects and attachment etc. is stopped. In this way, overall yoga practice saves energy. If you are experiencing problems/powerlessness in daily activities due to Kundalini contemplation, then you can stop thinking about it during the day, and the time of yoga practice and depth of meditation can also be reduced.

The colourful and strange types of collective singing, dancing and noise that are done in various religions, sects and traditions related to them; all that is done only for Kundalini awakening. Due to this, the vital energy of sound remains available to the Kundalini, due to which the possibility of its sudden awakening increases considerably, otherwise at least it gets strengthened. Premyogi Vajra also felt an increase in the strength and stability of his Kundalini through such ceremonies. Probably Kundalini awakening has been accepted in every religion, with different names and methods.

Like other experiences, spiritual experiences also grow when shared. When Premyogi Vajra shared his experience of momentary spiritual knowledge with everyone on online social sites, especially spirituality-related sites, he got the strength of Kundalini awakening from it. Society's bad habit of hiding spiritual experiences probably started in the Middle Ages, when heretics and intolerant people came to dominate real religion. But today nothing like this seems to happen in most places, and fast means of communication are also available everywhere. By sharing experiences, while the receiver gets a new experience, the sharer also gets a new experience from someone else in return. It seems that the good effects of Kundalini awakening/self-awakening continue in the subsequent births as well, as Rishi Patanjali has written about it/Samadhi. Similarly, it also appears that its evolutionary effect is recorded on the gene/DNA, which is then passed on to the next generation. For this reason, the children of Premyogi Vajra also started having some strange effects right from birth. All these things simply mean that the evolution of mankind continues towards liberation, and in the coming time, everyone's brain will become as advanced as the Kundalini-awakened brain.

Advaita is also of two types. First, in which deprivation and sorrow are rejected. There is relatively lack of practicality and worldliness in it, because both of these require absence. Second, in which deprivation and sorrow are also allowed to arise as per the circumstances; they are neither welcomed, nor ostracized/rejected, but one remains situated as witnesses towards them. It is relatively more practical and worldly. Therefore, worldly people and nature also indirectly help the seeker of this second group in the awakening of Kundalini, in return for his good behaviour and worldliness. This second type of Advaita mainly arises from Shavid.

In fact, the nostrils keep opening and closing alternately. For only a short period of time, both pores remain open equally. That time is best for practicing yoga, because meditation feels good at that time. It is said that at particular times of both evenings means dawn and dusk, both nostrils are equally open. To fulfil this purpose, Hath yogic activities like Anulom-Vilom Pranayam and Neti are also done. If the leg on the side where the nostril is closed is kept down during Siddhasana, then perhaps there seems to be some ease in Kundalini meditation. There is one more thing. At a particular time, when both the nostrils are open, the mind automatically remains in a state of peace and meditation, and at that time one automatically feels like doing yoga. If the nostrils are not working equally, then by inhaling from the nostril which is more open, the Kundalini on the Muladhar gets strengthened better. Although Premyogi Vajra did not care about all these things, and apart from simple Anulom-Vilom Pranayam, did not do any special activity. Despite this, his sudden Kundalini awakening seems to have been possible only through the power of sexual yoga.

Whatever is written in the mythological Puranas is true. For example, even if there is a description of a hundred yards tall king or a flying horse, it is still true. In fact, all things are possible within the soul. Because the description of the soul is the main focus in the Puranas, hence nothing described in the Puranas is false. There is not much flight of imagination in Shavid, although reality has definitely been painted with real and non-dual colours.

It seems that Kundalini Yoga Sadhana has been specially designed for those people who do not get the opportunity to do physical work continuously and tirelessly. The Kundalini of those who do tireless physical and mental labour gets strengthened on its own, especially if they keep taking the help of Karmayoga of Shavid etc. Same thing happened with Premyogi

Vajra also. Physical and mental labour continue to reinforce each other. This is also the secret of Kundalini Yoga, because both types of labour are done in it, which also enhance each other.

While doing Yoga Sadhana, one should inhale with the stomach only and not with the chest, because only by breathing through the stomach, appropriate pressure of pranavayu can be created on the lower chakras and a subtle type movement can take place on them. Belly breathing improves meditation, calms the mind, relieves stress and depression, and develops many divine and spiritual qualities. Besides, by breathing from the stomach, vital air is also absorbed well through blood circulation, which keeps the body and mind healthy. With this, the lack of oxygen is compensated by just a small number of breaths. Due to this, the breath itself becomes Yogic, that is, the breaths become long and deep. In the beginning, there may be some difficulty due to lack of practice, but later on, abdominal breathing starts to feel good, and the seeker starts taking this breathing most of the time, even when not doing sadhana. Due to this, the abdomen may appear somewhat enlarged and swollen, although this is a normal symptom.

After fatigue, if the Kundalini is strengthened inside the brain even a little by holding the breath for a while with Moolabandha and Uddiyana Bandha, then one gets immediate relief with joy. Additionally, breathing also becomes frequent, regular and deep. It should be thought that due to the bandhas, the life force of the entire body has been imposed on the Kundalini, that is, in a way, the entire body and mind have been imposed on the Kundalini, because in reality the entire body and mind are the expressed form of the life force. Another method is to look inside your body, through your mind, in any of your states, and consider that present state of yours to be similar to the same state of the non-dual subtle bodily being. Due to this Kundalini suddenly appears in the mind/brain. Then that Kundalini fire should be ignited with the help of inhales and exhales.

It is absolutely true that when Kundalini becomes active, an immense power starts flowing in the mind. Same thing happened with Premyogi Vajra. He even felt like plucking stars from the sky and bringing them back. He was in adolescence at that time and was unable to control his powers. He wanted to lead everyone on the straight path, having the ability to rule the entire world. To protect his body from the shocks of that power, he always kept doing some non-dual work, so that there would be a positive discharge of uncontrolled power. He could not sit idle even for a few moments. When he felt tired, he considered it better to rest in solitude than to talk unnecessarily. Because of this he also got many advancements and achievements. Due to the same power, he was able to bring Shavid into his personal life also. This means that without power even non-duality cannot be developed. Shakti is everything that is why Shakti has been given the form of mother in all religions, especially Hindu culture, because mother gives everything. Gradually, with increasing age, he became relaxed, and his strength/energy automatically came under his control. The second time, when his Kundalini became active again, by then he had crossed many stages of age. Even then his power was very strong, due to which he did many amazing things, but it was not the same as before. The body-mind instrument that holds that Kundalini power had become very old. Yet he gained great strength. Immediately after his Kundalini awakening, with the power available to him, he compiled and bookified this huge, emotional, linguistic, grammatical, cerebral and abstract written/felt word material. From this it can be inferred that immediately after the awakening of Kundalini, the sages have written Vedas and Puranas like this book. Only the great brain/mental power generated by Kundalini awakening enables such great and spiritual work to be done.

Even after enlightenment or Kundalini awakening, if the non-duality arising from them is forcefully suppressed, then those transcendental spiritual experiences begin to be rapidly forgotten, and doubts also arise regarding the salvation considered possible from them. Fire burns both those who have complete knowledge about fire and also those who do not. Similarly, illusion targets both the ignorant and the enlightened. Just like a person who knows about fire, is cautious of it, and does not want to get caught in its clutches; in the same way, the enlightened one who understands illusion well, remains cautious of it, and always tries to protect himself from it. If enlightened people were completely untouched by Maya; then people like Lord Krishna, Ram, and Buddha etc. would not have remained engaged in non-dual yoga practice throughout their life. In this way, when even after self-knowledge or Kundalini awakening one has to adopt non-duality, then why not directly adopt that non-dual attitude from the beginning, which never deceives; why run after enlightenment or Kundalini awakening, whose effect may even be destroyed without continuing the non-duality? Self-knowledge is considered necessary for liberation, but its long-term effect also depends on non-duality; because after some time self-knowledge is forgotten, and only non-duality remains. Then why not consider non-duality as directly necessary for liberation? Premyogi Vajra had practiced Shavid-Advaita for 20 years, only then he got the self-inspiration to make yogic efforts for Kundalini awakening. Even if Kundalini awakening had not occurred to him, it would not have made any difference to him, because only through Advaita he had started feeling liberation and satisfaction. In this way, there is benefit from non-duality. But if he had rejected Advaita and started a blind race only for Kundalini awakening or enlightenment, it was possible that he would have got nothing. In fact, most people do not achieve direct success by rejecting Advaita. Liberation from Advaita Dharana seems to be easy in both the situations, whether Kundalini awakening/enlightenment has taken place or not. It simply means that the primary objective of the seeker should be non-dualism/Karmayoga. Kundalini awakening or self-knowledge should be a secondary objective.

After Premyogi Vajra experienced the above glimpse of enlightenment, the entire world seemed bewildered to him. Most of the people were immersed in blind love and attachment towards the world and by imitating each others, they themselves had gone mad. Therefore, he remained quiet, isolated from everyone and cut off from the world. Therefore, it was natural that he would seek the least refuge in the world for the glitter of his mind, due to the fear of being deceived by the world. Even if he sometimes took refuge in the world, it was with the natural influence of non-dual enlightenment, but it appeared to be darkness to the common people. In fact, the soul which is the top light for the enlightened, is the darkest for the ignorant. So because of that fear, he had almost given up enjoying the world, especially in the company of ignorant people. In that situation, it was Kundalini who maintained the sparkle of consciousness in his mind and did not let him get discouraged from social life. She continued to guide and protect him properly.

Non-duality itself gives rise to non-attachment. When we hold any resolution of action with the help of meditation on Shavid, means with non-duality, at the same time that resolution of action, like the rabbit's horn, automatically disappears from the mind, that is, the attachment to it ends, or rather, the glue that connects that action-resolution with the mind dries up within a moment.

Due to the influence of continuous sex yoga; a sex yogi becomes calm like a child, pure, dazed, tired, non-dual, detached, full of mental Kundalini, carefree and blissful. His head seems empty, thoughtless and light. In the midst of that thoughtlessness, the shining Kundalini keeps emerging in his mind from time to time, which is probably the reason for his divine bliss. In such a situation, his Kundalini can awaken at any time after finding favourable conditions.

After some practice, at the time of Kundalini rotation, with the help of Bandhas, when the prana of the entire body is gathering above the Kundalini located on the chakra, then one should feel that the entire body and mind along with the prana have reached there. And by connecting with Kundalini, it has become one. Then while breathing normally, one should meditate that the Kundalini-volcano is flaring up by drawing the vital air. In fact, everything is a manifestation of Prana/life force. In fact, Vedic Havan was also performed to ignite Kundalini. In that, Kundalini was meditated in the form of fire-flame, flaring up with offerings (food/prana) and air (vital air). Besides, he also received all-round strength from various words, fragrances and musical tunes etc. Similarly, as soon as Kundalini starts appearing from the Advaita of Shavid, it should be ignited with the breath. Just as when a motor engine starts firing or there is an explosion of fire, air enters inside it rapidly and with a loud sound, in the same way, by meditating on Kundalini, the breath chasing it gets ignited. By meditating anywhere and continuously pouring breath on the Kundalini situated on the chakras, that Kundalini automatically rises to the level of chakra, and any meditation becomes Kundalini-like. Similarly, one should not think that he is meditating, but while paying attention to the long and deep breaths taken with the belly, one should maintain the belief that the breath itself is meditating on the Kundalini by falling on it. This also reduces the burden on the mind and does not create much difficulty.

Kundalini is a humanized body-being. She also breathes like us. Therefore we can see the Kundalini breathing and getting strengthened in the form of our breath on the Chakra.

Nowadays, mostly where there is hard work, there is no Advaita, and where there is Advaita, there is no hard work. In this way, according to the story of friendship between a blind man and a lame man, some societies are blind and some are lame. In fact, hard work and Advaita are complements of each other, which keep reinforcing each other. Without one quality, the other quality begins to deteriorate. If both come together, no one can stop Jivanmukti.

Moolabandha is like a level-regulator of the height of Kundalini. By pressing it a little more, the Kundalini rises a little, and by leaving it a little loose, the Kundalini descends a little. Its pressure is kept at such a level that the Kundalini remains on a specifically specified chakra.

It is said in every philosophy/religion that even after attaining enlightenment one should continue to live a non-dual life, only then enlightenment becomes firm in life, otherwise, it remains incomplete. Premyogi Vajra also observed that without consistent adherence to Advaita, self-knowledge also diminishes. The instincts of enlightenment or Kundalini awakening are also like other mental instincts, although they are comparatively much stronger, that is why they are remembered for a long time. But this does not mean that those instincts are never forgotten. The rule applies the same to all similar things. In fact, they too are forgotten, although after a much longer period of time than other ordinary mental states. This means that Advaita should always be followed. In fact, Advaita is everything. It is God. It is salvation. It is self-knowledge. It is Kundalini awakening. It is love. It is heaven. It is humanity. Advaita Vedanta also says the same. This philosophy considers Advaita as everything. This philosophy considers Advaita as the end of Veda, i.e. the essence of Veda. If non-duality is present in the mind; then resolutions and emotions emerge with great peace, comfort, love and joy. Many people may think that to create non-duality one does not have to put in any strength or make any effort. In fact, nothing is achieved without effort. One has to make continuous efforts to maintain non-duality continuously. To make the present situation non-dual, a momentary glance is cast at the Shavid philosophy or at one's own hand considering nondual body-beings situated everywhere inside it like him. It is like just as a driver casts a glance at the side mirror. Without taking his eyes off the road ahead or without turning his head, he casts a momentary and oblique glance at the mirror. In the same way, when the present mental state is superimposed over Shavid, the seeker takes a deep breath of relief and becomes situated in Advaita, due to which his Kundalini also gets exposed. It also does not badly affect the worldly situation just like proper driving of the driver is not disturbed. Apart from the body, an oblique mental gaze can also be cast towards the external nature or the gross world, because in Shavid we have already proved that "Yatpinde Tatbrahmande", i.e. non-dual body-country and non-dual body-persons residing in them are present at every place. The more often, more diligently and more skilfully one does this, the more benefits one gets. This has to be done again and again. With this method, as told above, his current reasonable state is also not affected, just as the driving ability of the driver is not affected. In fact, maintaining Advaita is as much an art as driving a vehicle. Most of the physical tasks are done by the body and naturally (habitually), for which there is no need for the mind to wander. If there are tasks in the mind like study or management etc., then if those tasks are completed as soon as there is non-duality present in the mind; one becomes free from the natural side effects of bondage, attachment etc. of the mind. Similarly, even a momentary glance towards the Kundalini dispels Dvaita, and the Kundalini gets exposed. Then she increases the breathing for her expression and makes it regular. The Kundalini fire flares up more and more with the inward breath, and with the outbreath, its smoke keeps coming out. After that sideways glance, there is no need to panic for some time; because then everything, even the so-called wrongful feelings like ego, restlessness, greed, attachment, etc. get transformed and become right and beneficial.

Nearing Kundalini awakening, Premyogi Vajra was also facing various virtual problems. Using 'Virtual' word because although those problems sometimes seemed real to him, but upon deep consideration, they were not problems but only facilities. He also became aware of the virtual economic problems. He also became aware of virtual enemies. He also became aware of virtual social problems. He also became aware of virtual family problems. He also became aware of virtual business problems. He also became aware of other virtual problems related to space and time. He also became aware of virtual emotional problems. This shows that Kundalini gets nourishment from problems, because being afraid of problems, man takes refuge in

Kundalini. If there are no problems in someone's life, then Kundalini creates unreal problems for its awakening. Because only a person who is afraid of problems leaves the world and depends on Kundalini; that is why when a person becomes busy in nurturing the Kundalini alone, then virtual problems automatically arise in his life. Those problems do not seem to him or sometimes seem to be minor, but to other people, seeing his loneliness, they really seem to be in his life. It is just like there is no tree in the mirror, but it appears to be.

One definitely gets the results of spiritual practice. If the result is not obtained soon, it will definitely be obtained sooner or later. Whatever amount of spiritual practice is done, one definitely gets that amount of results. In reality, the fruits of sadhana keep on accumulating and over time, they manifest themselves in the form of Kundalini awakening. Sadhana is only that in which there is meditation on Kundalini, no matter what type it may be. It can be of any type - Sandhyavandan Yoga, Karmayoga, Shavidyoga, Advaita Yoga, Bhakti Yoga, Gyan Yoga, Kundalini Yoga etc.

By adopting Advaita, one also looks like a drug addict. Even when he is awake, he seems to be sleeping. Even when he works, he looks workless. Despite being conscious, he seems unconscious. Even though he is alive, he looks as if he is dead. Even though he is healthy, he looks like a patient. Despite being active and fresh, he looks lethargic and tired. But in reality he is different from all these, like a divine man. He is with thoughts, but seems thoughtless. This is the state of non-duality mixed duality, which is also called the state of Dvaitadvaita (Trans state). There is presence as well as absence in it. In other words, there is neither presence nor absence in it.

During Siddhasana, when the right foot is kept down, the left foot keeps sliding downwards over the right leg. To avoid that slipping, the left leg has to fit properly into the crack of the folded right leg. Due to this, the round bones of both the feet may collide with each other, but gradually one gets used to it. Siddhasana should not be done forcefully and stubbornly, without practice, because this has damaged the knees of many yogis. The habit should be established gradually. If you feel uncomfortable in Siddhasana, then you can also do Ardha Siddhasana or simple asana. By the way, tension is felt on the knees even in Ardhasiddhasana. Therefore, the hips should be kept at some height with the help of a thin pillow etc., so that the legs are little downwards in the direction of the knees. It provides relief to the knees.

The feeling of witnessing and the feeling of nonduality, both these feelings should be together. If there is no feeling of non-duality, then the seeker remains stuck to only one witnessed feeling, due to attachment. To give momentum to the emotions, hence to the actions, hence to the life, the feeling of Advaita should also be there along with it. Without non-duality, Sakshikarana-bhava can be done, but without Sakshikarana-bhava, non-dualism cannot be easily imbibed. In fact, if we look deeply, both are the same thing.

In most of the places in the scriptures it is mentioned that this life is unreal, do not consider this world as true, etc., perhaps there is a hidden secret in it too. If someone, despite living life adequately, considers it unreal, then it is natural that he will remain detached from life. If someone rejects life fully considering it completely false, then he will not be able to live life. Nevertheless, now even scientists have started believing that this world is of unreal/3D simulation/virtual type. They are considering it to be a 3D game being played by alien beings in a giant computer. In reality, the space itself is the computer, and the gods inspired by supreme God are the gamers playing the game of the world.

The description that comes in the scriptures that one should avoid the attachment to women, is probably not from a direct point of view, but is only an indirect suggestion. This does not mean that you should stay away from the beautiful faces of women, their sweet voices or their feminine thoughts and behaviour. If this is done, then how will sexual stimulation be achieved, and if stimulation is not achieved, then how will Kundalini be able to get the liberating momentum for awakening? Its real meaning probably is that under the influence of excitement, do not make such close contact with women, due to which the Kundalini power goes out, or sociality is harmed; but remain moderate. Besides, there is also a fear of spread of many diseases due to close proximity of touch etc. It is also described in the Yoga Shastras that long-term practice of Yoga makes a person attractive, due to which he can fall in love with a woman. What this probably means is that the Kundalini which has attained strength automatically starts getting attracted towards sexual yoga for its awakening, as happened with Premyogi Vajra. But most of the yogis are not able to understand this, and they also do not get proper guidance from a qualified Guru etc., due to which there is a possibility of them becoming corrupt in yoga.

Kundalini Yoga probably works like a goldsmith's hammer. With his small hammer, the goldsmith gives the gold the required shape by hitting it slowly. Even soft gold can break due to blacksmith's heavy blows. In the same way, a Kundalini Yogi also gradually strengthens his Kundalini with small and regular practices every day and takes it to the height of awakening. According to this principle, the great yogi Shri Lahiri Mahashay also used to say about Kundalini Yoga, "Banat-Banat Ban Jaaye" means going and going fully goes. Just as by continuously and lightly hammering on a stone, it gradually becomes weak and finally breaks; in the same way, with light breaths, the Kundalini gradually gets strengthened and finally becomes strong. Just as the small and continuous blows of the engine's hammer (piston), driven by the power of air, rotate even the heavy tires of big vehicles, in the same way the breath putting a light and regular blow gradually exposes and shakes the suppressed Kundalini and makes it active. Just as a bulldozer gives a powerful push to the soil by moving back again and again, little by little, in the same way the mind and breath (breath) also push the Kundalini little by little moving back again and again. Live, so that by accumulating power again and again, they can push harder again and again and shake the Kundalini. If too much sadhana is done at once, it can have adverse effects on the soft mind of the yogi and hence on his life. That is why one should not hold the breath for too long on the chakra, otherwise it reduces the concentration power at that time, leads to sleepiness, suffocation, and may also have some long term side effects.

To get quick benefits from Kundalini Yoga, it is very important to have favourable conditions. Favourable circumstances are not achieved without God's grace available through devotion to God. If one takes the help of Shavid, then the best devotion to God happens every moment, because real devotion to God can happen only through Advaita. God has created non-dual humanoid beings only for the development of humanity. When a person practices Shavid keeping this in mind, then the best devotion is done automatically. Premyogi Vajra also got favourable conditions at the time of Kundalini awakening, probably due to the above mentioned reason. After

20 years of practice of Shavid-Puranas with reasonable humanity and hard work, when he suddenly got the opportunity of deep solitude, he himself got engaged in the search of Kundalini. Then, after about a year of research with the help of ordinary books and e-books, he himself got engaged in Kundalini Yoga Sadhana for direct experience of Kundalini. If he had delayed, his mind would have again been filled with worldly entanglements, as before, due to which he would not have been able to attain Yoga siddhi with that much ease. Therefore, it was only due to God's inspiration that he was able to take the right decision at the right time.

In reality, Guru Etc., whatever exists in the form of Kundalini of the seeker, he is not able to tell anyone about it, because that Kundalini is closest to his soul, and how can anyone tell his too much or say top personal matter to anyone? How can one say that he meditates on himself? The more difference/gap there is in one's mind between the observer (himself) and the observed (world/Kundalini), the more he trumpets it. When we say, "I love him", then we actually do not love him. When we truly love him; we cannot say this about him, because in true love, his picture gets firmly settled in our mind, and that lover becomes our own form. Only a mad person would say that I love myself. One who claims to be in love is not actually loved, and even if there is love, it is destroyed when it is declared. With repeated meditation on an object/person, conscious/pleasant love for it increases continuously, with this the Kundalini becomes the most beloved thing, off course in mind. This is the basic principle of Kundalini Yoga.

Many people think that joint families are better, and many think that dissolved families are better. In fact, both are better as per the requirement. It seems that at the time of development of Kundalini, for achieving high diligence, high love and high practicality along with Advaita, large families are beneficial. But for the ultimate nourishment of Kundalini and its awakening, small, peaceful and secluded families with little hard work and practicality are more beneficial. The above circumstances had happened in the same manner with Premyogi Vajra also.

Kundalini Yoga is actually a regulator and controller of the sexual power obtained under Sexual Yoga. While saving the sexual power, it directs it in the right direction, i.e. in nourishing the Kundalini. In fact, when a man becomes stressed and tired up due to various reasons, then his mind rushes towards sexual relations, so that he can gain power immediately. Although he generates that sexual power, but he is not able to consume it, and soon wastes it in the form of discharge. Instead of gaining power from it, the person also has to lose some of the old and accumulated power of the body. In fact, Kundalini is that conscious battery, which is able to store the sexual energy within itself and then releases it slowly, through which a man can perform many types of good deeds, even Kundalini-awakening and it also provides Enlightenment. With this power, Kundalini increases the self-control of the seeker, which also protects him from sexual crimes. At the time of sexual yoga, first of all, if Kundalini Yoga is practiced in any form for about 1 hour, then only perseverance is generated in Kundalini Samadhi, due to which the power of strong restraint is obtained, which makes sexual yoga successful. This means that a simple Kundalini Yoga practice in a single sitting should be for at least one hour, only then it can produce beneficial effects. By regularly practicing Kundalini Yoga in the morning and evening, all the activities and thoughts done during the day and night (dreams) automatically become non-dual. If in the beginning Kundalini rotation is done for a long time while being bound in the above mentioned Yum-Yum Aasana, then only sexual yoga becomes full of restraint, powerful, Kundalini nourishing and full of humanity. Kundalini also protects from sexual gluttony. If the sexual yoga partner is treated well during the practice, only then does she help in sexual yoga. Even in ordinary life, if any sensation arises on the Vajra and it expands, then practical Uddiyana Bandha should be applied, by pulling the body and prana upwards, so that the Kundalini located on the Vajra rises to the brain and starts developing there. Due to this, the vajra suddenly returns to its previous state, to its small size. By doing this repeatedly, the Kundalini becomes very strong in the brain. This is the secret of the Tantra, this is the secret of the Tantra. Due to this, Premyogi while being with first Devirani, would remain in the trance of her form, without her physical touch, only due to sexual excitement, as has been mentioned earlier in the book.

Astrology, Vaastu Shastra, etc., all the scriptures and hymns written related to various spiritual conducts and thoughts, all of them are mainly made to destroy attachment, hence they are in accordance with Shavid. With their help, no one can act as per their wish, due to which the avoidance of attachment happens automatically. In fact, attachment mostly happens in arbitrary actions. But the only possibility of harm from the above scriptures is that by adopting them without understanding them properly, the pace of work can become very slow, which can also hinder rapid and complete development. This does not happen with Shavid, because in it, any conduct can be done in any way as per the problem and as per the need, with humanity and in the interest of humanity. Advaita itself arises from the detachment created with the help of the above scriptures including Shavid, because someone's detachment towards the luminous world simply means that he does not consider his thoughtless and natural soul as less than anyone, that is, for him Emotions and lack of emotions, everything is equal.

The biggest and immediate benefit that Premyogi Vajra got from Kundalini awakening was that he got rid of the mental Kundalini in the form of Pratham Devirani, because in its place, the Kundalini in the form of his Guru started becoming established. Although this had started happening long before the awakening, after the awakening there was a sudden increase in it, an increase in trust in it and self-satisfaction in that regard. His new Kundalini (old spiritual man) was awakened only when his old Kundalini (first goddess) had become very weak with the ravages of time. This means that Kundalini awakening is a continuous and gradual cumulative process, not an instant or sudden process (on-off system). Earlier, Premyogi Vajra felt that it was the feminine nature due to which she loves her lover a lot and served him a lot that is why the mental picture of Devirani was doing him good in every way. He was not able to understand that doing this is the nature of any Kundalini, not only the Kundalini related to women. Although it is a different matter that due to the natural sexual attraction between a man and a woman, the mental Kundalini of the physical form of a woman is very strong in the mind of a man. He thought that when someone's mental picture was doing him so much good, then his actual physical form would do him even more good. That is why from time to time he used to yearn for the physical form auf the goddess. But in reality this does not happen. Only Kundalini can do such supreme good, not any physical form. Being ignorant of this principle, he started expecting more support from the physical form of his second wife than from the Kundalini of his first consort, and used to get angry again and again when the same did not happen. Later, when the physical form of the second goddess indirectly helped in the awakening of his Guru-Kundalini, he understood the whole thing. Then he saw that his Guru-Kundalini was doing him even better than his previous Devirani-Kundalini, because Guru-Kundalini was not creating excitement like Devirani-Kundalini, and was also not anti-social like her. In fact, by giving importance to the physical form of a woman, considering her as a goddess who provides love, well-being, good inspiration etc., she has been given the equivalence of mental Kundalini, because her actual physical nature is also similar to Kundalini, and she also helps the most in awakening Kundalini.

Advaita also increases the quality of work. Advaita automatically curbs wasteful mental tendencies. Therefore, the mental power that is saved by this is automatically used in increasing the quality of work. Along with this, Kundalini also gets strengthened. It was just like, "One work, two results".

Sometimes the author feels that this world runs according to the wishes of enlightened people also. When there is a need for a special change, then the eternal Mother Nature, by her power, provides favourable circumstances and makes a person enlightened. Because a self-enlightened person becomes self-fulfilled and fully accomplished with that, the Goddess forces him in many ways to make wishes. She creates virtual troubles, sorrows, pains etc. in his life; due to which he is forced to wish for the welfare of the world without any mental disorders. Nature then starts a campaign to fulfil his wish. What is said in the scriptures that the world is running only due to the will of Brahma, probably also reflects the wishes of the Brahmagyanis. It can also be said that Brahma makes his will manifest through Brahmagyanis also.

The author feels that it is probably from the shape and type of the vajra that the name Kundalini was born. As soon as the vajra is extended, the kundalini is placed on it. As soon as the vajra gets contracted and coiled slightly, the kundalini emerged from there and appeared in the brain through the bandhas. If one ever feel greedily sexual, he need not lose his enthusiasm. The running man can both slide down and get up again. One should always build sexual yoga devotion in mind and try to raise his soul. This proverb seems to be built in the context of concentrated meditation of Kundalini: "Eke sadhe sab sadhe, sab sadhe sab jaaye" means proving one, all is proved; proving all, all is lost. The name 'Kundalini' in the feminine seems to have been given because sexual attraction is the best samadhikaraka force, which is most likely to cause a woman to become a samadhi-kundalini, as the first goddess with simplicity had established herself in vajra's mind with ease and firmness.

It is said about the enlightened Sri Ramana Maharshi that once he had his tooth removed without any anaesthetic, which was natural to cause severe pain, but he did not feel the pain. Premyogi Vajra also had a similar experience. He was under the full influence of enlightenment at that time, because at that time less than 3 years had passed since he had experienced enlightenment (the full influence of enlightenment). The medicine had no effect in that too, due to which he suffered severe pain while pulling out the tooth. The dentist forcefully removed his tooth by pressing hard and ignoring his screams. But due to that pain, he did not feel even the slightest bit of any anger or disorder inside him. That pain also did not seem like pain to him, but felt like a normal feeling like other feelings. Due to this, non-dualism spread within him, and the clarity of remembering enlightenment also increased in his mind for some time. Besides, his Samadhi also became stronger. Although all these additional improvements were short-lived only.

Probably Premyogi Vajra could be successful in his Kundalini awakening even in a long period of 20 years because he was a veterinarian, and during those 20 years he continuously visited People's homes and offered his services to them in various matters related to their animals. Due to this, he always remained in the highest practicality, because due to this, he remained very close to the people of different areas. Being having in close contact to profession related to the body, Shavid itself remained constantly and firmly established in his mind. In this way we can see how great mental strength is required for Kundalini awakening. In this way, one can create one's own personal Advaita-philosophy, according to one's vocation. Since everyone wears the body, Shavid appears to be a personal philosophy for everyone.

Advaita arises from Kundalini because when we meditate on Kundalini, it fills our dark soul with its light. Due to this, we do not feel, or feel less difference, between ourselves (means soul/natural form of darkness/ absence) and the world (means mindfulness/light form/emotion form). In this way, when darkness and light seem to us to be the same form of light, then how can we perceive the difference among different lights (means among different mindfulness/feelings)? In the same way, due to that arising Advaita, when everything starts appearing to be the same, then why would there be any special attachment towards any particular object.

Kundalini-sensation is most powerful in the secret organs. That is why in sexual yoga the kundalini is imposed and meditated upon in every sensation of the body, especially in the secret sensations. Even in sexual attraction, the kundalini is most manifest in the genitals. Similarly, Kundalini Yoga is an artificial or man-made or less powerful sexual yoga.

For spiritual success, a lot of satvik and divine qualities like determination, dedication, enthusiasm, restraint etc. are required; just as to establish a big worldly industry, these qualities are required. Therefore, attention should also be paid to worldly achievements, because through them these qualities are developed, which help a lot in achieving spiritual success in future.

In between yoga, the mind should be allowed to wander a little here and there (towards various noises, songs and talks etc.), but the force of life should remain on Kundalini only. Due to this, the mind, taking with itself the power generated through these worldly acts, immediately falls on the Kundalini, and makes it shine.

When Premyogi Vajra himself spent a long time practicing practical Advaita, he seemed to be transformed, and his practical Advaita also automatically transformed into impractical or intense Advaita. Due to this, at first he became studious, in which he read only books related to Yoga etc. Then satisfied, he started practicing yoga. In between, he automatically got attracted towards sexual yoga, and started reading subjects related to it. Then, by putting into practice all the relevant subjects read in those books, he became proficient in Kundalini Yoga mixed with sexual yoga. Meanwhile, his Kundalini awakening also took place.

Earlier in this book, the author has proved through the experience of Premyogi Vajra that Advaita and Kundalini co-exist, hence by meditating on Kundalini at any time, Advaita automatically arises. This is such a simple and indirect method to create non-duality or to bind the mind, just like not tying the whole elephant, but tying only its leg, by which the whole elephant itself gets easily tied. Therefore, through yoga practice, one should meditate on Kundalini every day.

If the Kundalini is flaring here and there from the Chakra, then it should be considered as the flame of the Kundalini fire situated in that Chakra, even if that flame is downwards, and even if it is upwards, even if it reaches the head. Because within a short time the Kundalini itself reaches the origin of its flame i.e. the basic chakra (where it is being meditated at that time). During Yogasana, while breathing into your lungs, you can feel the joints mainly chakra-joints or bends of the body moving slightly as if those joints are breathing inwards, and the Kundalini being meditated there can be felt. When yogis practice Kundalini Yoga for 1-1.5 years, then many a times, while standing, sitting or even sleeping, they unintentionally maintain the position of their body which causes blissful type pain in various joints. Any, especially the waist joint (in the back, directly opposite the Svadhisthana chakra) should become more and more clear, and along with it, the Chakrasana Kundalini located on it. Due to the clarity of that joint and the changing position of the breaths, and due to the changing pressure or movement on the same joint, those breaths also keep hitting there easily, due to which those breaths also keep provoking the Kundalini. Since blood vessels and nerves are present together, it is natural that when the sensory vessels become active due to bending or movement of the joints, then due to pressure etc., the blood vessels also become active. The prana flowing through the same blood vessels, along with that sensation, also strengthens the Kundalini located at the place of sensation (chakra etc.), in the same way as by irrigating the grass, the insect situated above it is also irrigated. It happens on its own. During Yogasana, the main aim should be only to meditate on Kundalini and not to do physical exercise. Therefore, instead of making the asana the best, the focus should be on Kundalini. The quality of the asana keeps increasing along with the quality of the Kundalini itself. The quality of the asanas can also be given attention, although along with the Kundalini, not at the expense of the quality of the Kundalini. Premyogi Vajra also did very simple types of physical exercises in the form of yoga. In fact, any physical exercise (especially stretching exercises) if done in the form of yoga, becomes yoga. By doing Kundalini Yoga in the evening, the stress of the day calms down. After that, one should have food and drinks, and after that for light entertainment, one should listen to music or watch television (news) etc. If no more stressful work is done after yoga, then the whole night is spent peacefully and happily.

If the human form of a beloved person or deity is not meditated upon in a concentrated form by giving it the form of Kundalini, then how can various human expressions and mental states be superimposed on Kundalini? If such implantation is not done on the Kundalini, then how will the Kundalini become progressively stronger? In fact, at the time of anger, that humanized Kundalini also looks like an angry man. Through this the seeker becomes aware of his anger and he then controls it. The same should be understood with other expressions also. Similarly, continuous meditation seems to be possible or accessible only through humanized Kundalini, because such meditation is also acceptable in the society, hence it also gets indirect social strength (means strength of recognition). If one constantly meditates in one's mind on a luminous dot or a shining bell, where will the society approve of it? In Premyogi Vajra, Kundalini formed in the form of the first goddess; so almost the entire society happily accepted it, except the section trapped in bigotry, jealousy, ego, duality and attachment. If he had proved Kundalini in the form of a shining rock, how would most of the society accept it? From this it appears that love for humanity is everything.

When mastery over Prana is achieved, then it appears that the meditation of Kundalini is not being done by the mind but by Prana. That is, the burden of applying the mind becomes a little lighter, and like before, there is no need to apply it forcefully.

Premyogi Vajra was also an investigative-scientist type of person. Once he wanted to know whether one could be saved from the bondage of karma only with the help of self-knowledge. To search for it, he left the good company and took with him the feeling of attachment and duality and jumped into this deep world-ocean, although the indirect and slight influence of Shavid was strongly helping him. Anyway, at that time almost eight years had passed since he had experienced enlightenment, and the memory of enlightenment had also become very blurred or almost destroyed in his mind. In this way, without the life supporting jacket of non-attachment and non-dualism, within 3 years he became self-deluded and started drowning in the ocean of the world. He had almost completely forgotten enlightenment. He understood that enlightenment alone cannot do anything if non-dualism and non-attachment are forcibly abandoned. Therefore, knowing this, he started trying to get out of that dark ocean with the direct help of Shavid. With the help of that good effort, it took about 12 years of well-demonstrated Tantric-Karmayoga for him to become capable of coming out completely. After so many years, when he became tired of Tantric Karmayoga, he went for a retreat; then gradually, within a year or six months, the remaining dust of mild confusion that had settled on his mind was cleared to a great extent. The dust of self-delusion definitely accumulates through action, no matter if that action is done with the Tantric-Karmayoga method, although that dust is comparatively very thin, and the dust also disappears soon. Then he again started feeling the same liberation as he had felt after the momentary self-knowledge, although he did not remember the self-knowledge at all. Along with this, he also experienced Kundalini awakening. This proves that enlightenment alone cannot do anything, but it is also necessary to have non-duality and non-attachment. Self-knowledge only motivates people to adopt Advaita and non-attachment by telling them the salvation-like benefits of adopting it. This also proves that maintaining non-duality is more important than self-knowledge, and even if non-duality and detachment are maintained without self-knowledge, liberation still seems possible. Similarly, when it is said that a wife automatically gets the result of liberation by serving her husband, it also means that liberation does not require self-knowledge, but only a non-dual approach. A devoted woman herself gets that perspective through the company of her husband.

The Gita also mainly praises detachment. "You have right to action only, never to fruits, do not be the cause of the fruits of action, do not be attached to inaction. 'Karmanye vadhikaraste' and 'ma karmaphalaheturbhuh', both combined, mean directly that one should also keep doing work, and not consider oneself as the cause, i.e., the doer, of the fruit of action. Such a situation is possible only if karma is done with detachment. 'Ma sangostvakarmani', means that even if action less states occur in the middle of actions, due to rest etc., one should not be attached to them. If we go deeper, the whole verse means that the thought of the fruit is not to be abandoned so that the action is ill-effected, but to be abandoned so that the action is not ill-effected. This is possible only if the fruit is thought of or consumed with detachment. While doing the karma, it is natural that the thought of the fruit will come to mind. If a farmer plants a pomegranate orchard, he will have thoughts about the pomegranates produced, their market values and the dividends he will receive. In fact, he will only plant a garden motivated by fruit-gain. If he does not discuss the fruit, he will suffer loss. Therefore, the meaning of this verse here seems not to be to renounce the thoughts of fruit, but to hold a sense of unattachment to thoughts of fruit. The statement of not having rights about the fruit is only to produce detachment from the fruit. At the same time, if he will not have any thought of the fruit, then he will not be able to work properly, which will break the second passage, "Ma sangostvakarmani", because then he will become attached to inaction. If there is attachment to inaction, then actions will not be performed, or they will be adversely affected, which will also refute the passage 'karmanyevadhikaraste'. "Ma karmaphalaheturbhuh" means that you should not think of yourself as the cause (cause) of the fruit of action or the one who produces it or the doer of the action. This also does not seem to mean that you should not think of yourself as the doer, but rather that you should think of yourself as the doer with detachment. Because if he does not consider himself the doer, he will not be able to do quality action with his mind, which will again break the above passage. In fact, all actions done and thought of with detachment are self-consumed, that is, they are not actions even though they are actions. Similarly, fruits thought or enjoyed with detachment cease to be fruits. If he understands that only the non-dual nature is the doer, not I, then he will not work, and will sit on the support of nature. The benefit of detachment is that even if for some reason he does not get the fruit, he does not attain the binding suffering, that is, his Advaita is not broken, because of his detachment, he has neither done karma, and therefore nor enjoyed their fruit, because how fruit without action. Even if the fruits are obtained, they are fruitless when enjoyed with detachment, that is, the same Advaita in both states. If he enjoys the fruit, it is still useless, and if he does not enjoy it, it is still useless. Anyway, Advaita and Anasakti are always together. For example, the farmers of Dehdesh continue to do karma. Many times they bear fair fruit, and many times their produce is destroyed by wild beasts, militants, or all victim to natural disasters and rebels. He does not suffer from the binding sorrow arising from duality, because he has always been non-dual, and has never developed attachment. No action is possible without fruit. At least we get the fruits of our actions in the form of humanity. If someone has to do attachment, he will also do it in the form of humanity (means in attainment of healthy body, its maintenance and basic activities). If someone does not want to get attached, he will not do so even for the biggest rewards. It all depends on perspective. The above description is not just from the book, but Premyogi Vajra had experienced everything himself.

Kundalini, strengthened by continuous morning and evening practice, works as a balancer/buffer, which protects the seeker from the shocks of change/duality, like shavid. These duality shocks keep damaging the soul.

Great people are not bound by religious, cultural, geographical and racial boundaries. They are global and even universal. Therefore they should be protected. There works and creations should also be protected. They can belong to any field. They can be scientists, yogis, tantrics, philosophers, artists etc., anything. Just as science gave Premyogi Vajra the strength to move towards self-knowledge, in the same way it can give it to others and future generations too. Just as he saw philosophy in science, similarly others and future generations can also see it. Just as Premyogi Vajra got the opportunity to learn Tantra Yoga from books and e-books, and awaken Kundalini through it, similarly others and future generations can also get the opportunity from his book. Just as he got help from various e-social sites, forums and blogs, similarly others and future generations can also get help. Therefore, all knowledge and techniques should be preserved for the future.

Just as the hot air inside the balloon, which raises the balloon to the heights of the sky, is not felt by anyone except that balloon itself; Similarly, no one can know the Kundalini residing in the mind of a person except that person, who is carried by it through the path of material progress as well as to the spiritual peak.

Kundalini can be given a rotation in times of stress, depression, fatigue, or in any state of free time. This refreshes the mind completely and mental defects are also eliminated. For that, first of all, by meditating on Kundalini in Swadhisthana and Muladhar, it is stimulated a little with the life force. Then by holding the breath, Moolabandha and Uddiyana Bandha are applied. Kundalini automatically rises from those bandhas and reaches the brain/Sahasrara. Then, while breathing regularly, it is meditated on in the mind for some time with some help from the breath. Then, when the brain starts feeling too heavy, then the Kundalini is brought down from the front chakras (suddenly or by meditating, as per convenience), to the navel chakra. Then all the defects are calmed down, and the person becomes completely refreshed. In fact, one of the shortcomings of practical Kundalini Yoga has been filled by the Tao-specified microcosmic orbit of Tao based on it. In Yoga, it is not said that Kundalini should be brought down from Sahasrara. Probably this was right for the Naishtika Yogi, because he had to prove only Kundalini awakening quickly, while staying away from public behaviour. Although a practical person has to keep many things in mind. He cannot bear the pressure of the brain, continuously.

At the time of pure mental love for the first goddess, when the Kundalini of her form was continuously burning with full intensity in the mind of Premyogi Vajra, at that time also he was going through a phase of transformation. All the past things and incidents were fading in his mind. His attachment and ego towards them was also diminishing. It seemed as if they were all moving away from the distance. Despite being there, they seemed as if they were not there. It seemed as if she was never physical, but was purely mental. All of them were appearing in the mind with a divine joy, and were also gradually diminishing. The Kundalini of that first goddess was dominating all of them. All of them were becoming secondary in front of that burning Kundalini, just as a lamp becomes secondary in front of the Sun. With all of them, that Kundalini was getting stuck. It seemed to Premyogi Vajra as if all those past things and events were from some of his past lives, when he was born in a spiritual family, but then he was reborn in a scientific family related to the goddess queen. To many people, especially those in the field of study, it seemed strange. Therefore, forgetting his old life, he started studying science whole-heartedly, due to which he got many successes. Probably this is what is called self-transformation or second birth. Then after about 20 years, he had his third birth, when in his mind, the Kundalini of his Guru was awakened. In him, to replace the first Kundalini (means First Goddess) of his mind, his second Kundalini (means Guru) had come, because that second Kundalini, after awakening, had become more powerful than the first Kundalini.

In the above mentioned case, just as Premyogi Vajra found the mental form of his Guru to be more true and direct than his physical form, in the same way any mental experience can be made direct or like physical. This means that all mental experiences are true. This also means that all the forms of Gods and Goddesses like Shiva, Vishnu, Krishna, Ram, Durga etc. are true, and Yogis have been experiencing them directly since ancient times. At the time when Premyogi Vajra saw the form of the Guru present in his mind (at the time of Kundalini awakening), at that time, naturally, he also experienced the visible scene in front of him as in his mind; because two completely identical experiences cannot be divided in such a way that one is external and one is internal. In fact, we call only those experiences as internal, which are secondary and of lower intensity than the external experiences. From this perspective, both the external and internal experiences seemed to him to be within himself, because he could not consider the mental form of his Guru as external, who was not even there, and had also become a resident of the divine world about 20 years ago. It was as if the sounds etc. happening at that experience-place did not come into his experience, except for the strange noise inside the brain, as has been described earlier also. Probably the priority of the brain is to maintain the visuals, the turn of sound comes only after that. At the time of that huge experience, all the brain's power was being used to maintain that powerful, physical/visual experience, and even that was falling short. Probably due to the flood of neurochemicals in the brain, the noise like the aforesaid manner was being produced.

Sometimes even the nails of Premyogi Vajra's toes would be uprooted. Neither any pain, nor any disease. The entire nail gradually turned white, and the top remained rough edged, due to which it had to be cut. Many times, a small part of it remained stuck somewhere, which had the redness of life. That part had to be left as it was, uncut. It is described at many places that due to yoga or active Kundalini, heat increases in the body, especially in the toes, due to which this happens. Perhaps that is why in the scriptures it is said to touch the toes of the Guru's feet, because the power of Kundalini is easily obtained from there.

After the above mentioned momentary enlightenment, probably Premyogi Vajra was not getting the strength of Advaita, because at that time he was also lacking in work. He was living a life of exile, away from his home. There, that village-accustomed Premyogi did not get the opportunity to work in the fields, barns etc. At that past village-time there was no trend of reading different books, nor were modern facilities like e-books, internet etc. available. In reality, Advaita/Dvaitadvaita arises from actions, especially actions involving physical labour and best of all from those actions in which both mind and body are used equally. It is through Advaita that Kundalini enters the Sushumna, due to which best stability is achieved. If non-dual actions are not available with intensity and continuity, then Kundalini does not get sufficient strength of non-duality. Due to this, it is not able to remain constant in the mind, which seems little painful after the supreme mindset of enlightenment or Kundalini awakening. Even if there is a lot of work, but Advaita is not adopted along with it, even then the full benefit is not achieved, although a little bit of Advaita is automatically found in a loving and emotional society. Due to lack of Advaita, Kundalini disappears completely in the state of absence/zero, which becomes little unbearable for a perfect Yogi. That situation is called the entry of Kundalini into Pingala or some say muladhara. In such a situation, the Yogi becomes greedy for his deeds and begins to sink into depression, due to which normal social behaviour and work gets adversely affected. Similarly, in the state of presence/non zero, Kundalini becomes very intense. It is called the entry of Kundalini into Ida Nadi (experiential). Even in such a situation, the mind becomes completely a slave of Kundalini and remains engrossed in the bliss of Kundalini, and is unable to pay proper attention to social behaviour and responsibilities. Due to non-duality, Kundalini remains almost equally present in feelings and absences, due to which protection is provided from the powerful shocks of duality. Due to duality of any level, shocks are bound to occur, however due to duality with Kundalini, those shocks can get amplified, due to which the possibility of loss can also increase. Advaita also gets enhanced by Kundalini, if it is well maintained. According to Advaita, when the Kundalini remains in almost the same state in all the states, then it is said that the Kundalini is situated in the Sushumna Nadi. In reality, nothing exists in absence, but still, due to Advaita, that absence does not become painful, nor does it last for long, because Kundalini soon reaches there with strange expressions. That feeling of Kundalini is also as addictive as any other feeling, although with the help of Advaita, that feeling is experienced in a dream like manner or in such a way that it does not cause shock in case of absence. Moreover, that feeling also does not last long, but soon there is absence. In this way, feelings and absences keep coming and going very quickly, due to which there is not enough time for attachment to occur. Therefore, there is protection from the duality caused by attachment. Now it has also been proven by science that half of the brain remains strong in emotions and the other half in absence. Half of it is controlled by Ida Nadi, and the other half by Pingala Nadi. When both Ida and Pingala nadis are of equal influence, then Sushumna nadi is said to be effective. Ida is connected to one nostril and Pingala is connected to the other. Sushumna becomes effective only when both nostrils are equally open. Anyway, due to the Advaita of Shavid, both the nostrils themselves remain open most of the time, as experienced by Premyogi Vajra. It also increases the qualities of a man like beauty, sociability, discharge of responsibilities and creativity etc. It is also seen practically that a person breathing from one nostril, making a sound or even indicating obstruction from the other nostril, seems somewhat strange. Most of the time, one's unequal nostrils are detected on one's own, through some divine intuition/or his duality. This proves that only non-dual people are more beautiful and attractive. According to phonetics means svar vigyan, nostrils are related to health. The author also found this to be true, when due to minor mental/physical illnesses and vaccinations, the movement of his nostrils seemed to change for a few days. It is also said that if both the nostrils remain equally open continuously for a few days, then enlightenment is achieved. In fact, this happens only when Advaita becomes very strong through repeated practice and not by the nostrils opening on their own by some miracle or tactic, like through artificial methods, such as yoga etc. By opening the nostrils with such tactics, some sense of non-dualism is generated, but real and solid non-dualism is generated only through the mind with the mixed help of non-dual scriptures and actions like that of Shavid-Puraan etc. When Advaita becomes very strong through repeated practice, the nostrils may be open on their own by some body-physiology and not by any miracle etc.

At the time of Kundalini awakening, Premyogi Vajra had experienced that he had completely become Kundalini-ego. The scenes that were in front of him also got connected with his that Kundalini-identity. This means that whatever was the experiential object at that time, it seemed to Premyogi Vajra as his own form, there was no difference between outside and inside etc. There is one more thing. If he had already kept in his mind that he would do this or that at the time of Kundalini awakening, then probably Kundalini awakening would not have happened, because it happens only when there is no possibility in the mind about its happening, and it has been kept without any preparation. That means it happens suddenly. This means that whatever the seeker does at the time of Kundalini awakening, he will do it naturally and without thinking. Perhaps only when the non-dual nature has matured, Kundalini can be fully tolerated.

Everyone's mental beliefs and ways of life are different. Therefore, the same sadhana method for everyone is not very effective. Vedas and Puranas are common to all, and are related to almost all the concepts and lifestyles, but still it is more effective to enrich them with the specific Advaita system related to it for a specific way of life. Premyogi Vajra had also done the same, due to which he was able to get success soon. According to the profession, Private Advaita Shastra can also be made. According to different professions, different non-dual concepts can be maintained in the mind. For example, if one's business is full of practicality, worldliness, etc.; so he can get maximum benefit from Tantra and along with it, Advaita Shastra based on that profession. Shavid encompasses all professions within itself, hence this Advaita Shastra can prove beneficial in every case. If there is a high proportion of sexuality in one's business or lifestyle, one can get more benefits from sex yoga with Shavid. If someone's business is full of idealism, moralism, rule-following, discipline, penance, sense control etc.; so simple Yoga, Bhakti, Gyan Yoga etc. along with Shavid can prove to be more beneficial for him. Nevertheless, as per interest, help of any spiritual practice or Advaita Shastra can be taken. A lot also depends on perspective. Premyogi Vajra's outlook had become Shavid-compliant, Tantra-compliant and sex-yoga-compliant in his teenage years, only then in his later years, he experienced Kundalini awakening through these sadhana methods. This proves that the sooner the foundation of spiritual perspective is laid in life, and continuous efforts are made to increase the spiritual practice related to that perspective, the sooner and greater the benefit one gets in the future. From the viewpoint of Tantra, Sexual Yoga and Shavid, Premyogi Vajra attained Kundalini awakening in just 20 years, that too with high quality deeds, lifestyle, facilities, worldliness and practicalities. Then there is no better viewpoint than this anywhere in sight. He experienced Kundalini awakening only through one year of regular Kundalini Yoga and in the last phase, additional one month of Sex Yoga. This is a surprise, because it is said that even regular practice of yoga takes many years. It took Shri Gopikrishna 17 years. Premyogi Vajra probably did it quickly because his basic spiritual approach (Advaita) was very old, and he had taken a lot of help from Shavid.

After Anulom-Vilom Pranayama, if you wait for a short time (about 15-20 minutes), the closed nostrils open on their own, and air starts flowing equally from both the nostrils. Doing yoga at that time gives special benefits. Therefore, the remaining yoga can be completed in the second sitting also.

The author remembers an incident. A famous and accomplished Tantric used to visit that area every year. Once he was roaming in the streets of the colony there. Everyone, especially the women, had closed the doors of the house from inside out of fear, because he knew hypnotism. An unwary man peered into the eyes of the Tantric through the window. He picked up his purse and opened the door latch and went out and gave his purse to the Tantric. When he came back inside, his wife scolded him severely, but he was hypnotized. So his wife herself came out, and without even looking at the Tantrik's eyes, she freed the purse, and then ran inside her room and locked the door again. That Tantric started calling loudly and lovingly with addresses like son, daughter etc. Her hypnotized husband came out again. Then tantric shown him his consecrated vajra and gave him a thread to tie on his too. In fact, the approach of common people towards sex is physical, whereas the approach of Tantric is spiritual. No one from that colony got angry with that Tantric, because they knew that Tantric are like that. Undoubtedly, Tantric may be wrong in the eyes of the world, but they are right in their own eyes and in the eyes of divine truth.

Achieving happiness through mental Kundalini awakening means that bliss lies only in the world inside the brain and not in the physical world outside. That is why Vedas, Puranas etc. are made in the form of entertaining stories.

It is said that love cannot be created by force, but the experience of Premyogi Vajra says that Tantra has the power to create love. On the strength of the aforesaid tantric connection with the first goddess, Premyogi Vajra had developed love for his guru, the old spiritual man who lived with him. Although it is generally seen that most of the people do not like the elderly, but Tantra had also destroyed that great interest barrier.

It seems that the more intense, powerful, shocking, joyful and experiential the experience of Kundalini awakening is; The more benefit one gets from it; Because in reality, that Kundalini picture should settle in the mind continuously, and it is often seen in the world that the stronger the experience, the more it settles in the mind.

The practice of worshiping Shaktipeeth, Bhagwati and Goddess Mata etc. is also according to Tantra. This practice teaches us to adopt the spirit of Tantra indirectly, because in a polite society it is considered rude to talk about Tantra directly. In fact, worship of Mother Goddess awakens respect for women. The spirit of tantra is strengthened by having respect for the woman, because without a tantra-oriented married life, the Kundalini-enhancing power of the body starts getting misused, due to which the wife becomes deprived of her role as an omnipotent mother, and due to which, seeing his own loss, the husband becomes showing less respect her. The feeling of respect towards her starts decreasing. Then as per the religious tradition, to re-awaken the feeling of respect towards the wife, the couple, especially the husband, automatically starts moving towards Tantrabhava.

It is said that celibacy leads to knowledge. In fact, most of the people do not have the knowledge of real celibacy, because real celibacy lies in Tantra only, but they think the opposite. If knowledge could be obtained only through sexual aversion, then children and the sexually disabled would be supremely intelligent. If knowledge could be obtained only through sexual aversion, then sexual yogis would not have got it at all, but the reality is that sexual yoga is the best means of knowledge. In fact, the more the production of sexual fluid and the more its conservation, both together, the stronger celibacy will be considered. This proves that the pinnacle of sperm production and the pinnacle of sperm conservation, both together become the pinnacle of celibacy. If Kundalini also joins with it, then it becomes the pinnacle of Yoga.

When Kundalini appears on the chakra, then it should be strengthened directly and with life. By the way, by meditating on the impact of breath on Chakrabindu, Kundalini itself appears there. Along with meditation on Kundalini, attention should also be paid to healthy and strong breathing in between. Due to this the Kundalini automatically shines more. But many times, by leaving the Kundalini and concentrating on the Chakra-point, that Kundalini also disappears. Although if it is unmanifested, then by meditating on the chakra-point it also becomes visible. One should not go into too much depth regarding the methods of asanas or pranayams. The main aim should be to meditate on the favourable chakras and Kundalini. Doing Kundalini Yoga in between work also gives a lot of strength to the Kundalini. Due to this, the mental energy acquired through sex gets applied to the Kundalini and keeps strengthening it. If once you focus/target your breaths on the Kundalini and strengthen it by paying attention to your deep breaths, then those breaths automatically continue to reach the Kundalini. If a person is very tired, and he meditates on the Kundalini at Mooladhar while taking quick, long breaths (like Kapalbhati), then that Kundalini appears blurry in the beginning. It means that there is a lack of vital air in the body. Then gradually the clarity of Kundalini increases, which means that the lack of vital air in the body is being compensated. At last the Kundalini becomes bright and clear with joy, which means that the lack of vital air in the body has been compensated. Then breathing also starts moving slowly and also becomes shallow. In this way, Kundalini is also a mirror of the available amount of vital air. By the way, after deep mental fatigue, if Kundalini is meditated, then suddenly Kundalini flares up, fatigue is eliminated, stress is reduced, lack of vital air is not felt, and breathing becomes very slow and almost stops. This means that the lack of Kundalini is more responsible for the mental fatigue at that time and the physical stress arising from it, rather than the lack of vital air.

Kundalini awakening is not a miracle or any special thing. This is just remembering a loved one or an acquaintance. When the depth of that blissful remembrance crosses a certain limit, then the same remembrance becomes Kundalini awakening. In reality, only the person, God etc. who is remembered becomes Kundalini. In fact, there is no difference between remembrance and Kundalini awakening; the only difference is in the depth, amount of joy and emotion. In Kundalini awakening, the depth of remembrance, joy and non-duality are almost at their peak; whereas in ordinary memory these three qualities are present in small quantities. With a single effort, no person can reach the depth of remembrance at which that remembrance becomes Kundalini awakening. That is why Kundalini Yoga Sadhana has been created, through which a particular person or a particular deity can be remembered again and again. Over time, the result of all the efforts being made over a long period of time can appear together at any time in the form of Kundalini awakening. Kundalini water gradually heats up, and finally boils and erupts in the form of Kundalini awakening. After that the Kundalini water cools down again and takes a lot of time to boil again. Just as water does not boil straight away, in the same way Kundalini awakening also does not happen suddenly or without prior preparation.

A large part of Premyogi Vajra's life was spent in the beauty of the mountains. Most of the times in the mountains, there are very sharp shocks of weather, which we also call in common language as dual feeling of cold and heat. It seems like it is a common thing there to be extremely hot during the day and extremely cold during the night. Even because of that, the sensitive Premyogi Vajra suffered a lot of mental trauma. But after taking shelter of Shavid's powerful Advaita, his troubles were greatly reduced, and at the same time, his Kundalini was also getting strengthened. In such changing circumstances, Shavid works very quickly as a panacea for the disease of Dvaita, because it is proved that Dvaitadvaita is the real Advaita, and also that the more Dvaita, the greater is the benefit of Shavid produced Advaita. In the mountains, there are many duality-shocks of this type and also of other types that is why there one gets results very quickly from non-duality. Probably that is why the mountains are called Tapobhoomi. Although in the end, one has to leave duality completely, adopt peace and engage in yoga practice with full devotion, only then Kundalini awakening takes place. In fact this happens automatically.

Yogi also learns non-attachment through Kundalini meditation. A particular deity or individual is established as the Kundalini of the seeker only if there is no attachment towards him. The functioning of the body is adversely affected by obsessive thinking, hence one cannot continuously meditate on a picture with attachment to it in one's mind. Similarly, by forceful and continuous meditation on the Kundalini picture, the attachment towards it automatically gets destroyed, so that the body can be protected from the side effects caused by attachment. Also, because in the form of Kundalini picture, there are transcendental persons mostly like Gods, Gurus etc., hence it is natural to have non-attachment towards them. Due to this, the seeker comes to know the importance of non-attachment in his daily life and he automatically starts adopting it.

By reading interesting books, especially imaginary and spiritual books like Puranas etc., the Kundalini picture of the mind gets superimposed on their stories etc. Due to this the Kundalini gets strengthened continuously. If such events are seen and heard in real visual form on television, radio etc., then the same does not happen, because then the directly seen pictures dominate the Kundalini picture of the mind, due to which the Kundalini disappears from the mind.

All the things and incidents described in this book seem both real and imaginary to Premyogi Vajra. Likewise, they sometimes seem real to him; and sometimes imaginary like a dream, imaginary especially in the physical environment and materialistic/dualistic state of mind. Even most of the people associated with these facts and events may consider them to be mere imaginations. They would probably be the same people who do not understand the immense empire of the mind, and consider gross materiality as everything. There are plenty of such people these days. People who look into the depths of the mind are rare these days. All these mental phenomena, which are brighter, clearer and more real than the physical form, are the result of non-duality and non-attachment achieved through Guru's grace and Shavid thinking.

Duality-nonduality viewpoint is the viewpoint of the subtle physical person. In fact, real Advaita arises from Dvaitadvaita (dvaita+advaita). The meaning of Dvaita or duality of Dvaitadvaita here is to accept all reasonable/ natural human emotions and actions as they are in their changing form; and the meaning of its Advaita part is to experience oneself unaffected by changing emotions and actions. By practicing non-dualism directly, duality is maintained, because voluntary non-duality gets nourishment from duality only, that is, in a way, there is duality. Like Dehpurush, both Dvaita and Advaita should be adopted together, because by this both are destroyed, just as by mixing + 1 and - 1, both are destroyed. From this, self-evident, natural, indescribable and blissful Advaita automatically arises. If both Dvaita and

Advaita are denied, then the man will become stagnant, contrary to the nature of the work-minded body-kingdom, because like the world of physical body, duality and non-duality are also necessary for gross worldly activities too. Advaita is the natural religion of the entire nature along with the humanoid body-being. Because there is no difference in soul form between the body-being and all other natural objects, hence it is proved that the real soul-form of all the natural objects in the universe is duality. The ocean never changes with the change in its water level. Similarly, the Sun never changes with the change in its level of brightness. Like the water level of the ocean, the mental level of a man should also keep changing, only then he will get the opportunity to implement Advaita, because who will say that the ocean is non-dual if its water level remains the same. If a man, in the name of Advaita, tries to forcefully stop the oscillations of the mind and keep the mind in a constant state, then he will not get the opportunity to imbibe the non-duality achieved by thinking about the body-country, and along with that, his work will also be affected or hampered. Real Advaita is that which arises spontaneously and with blissful emptiness after continuous and long-term efforts of Dvaitadvaita. For example, in the group of friends of Premyogi Vajra's consort, there were goddesses of different colors. Although Premyogi Vajra understood the difference between everyone very well, he did not reveal it to anyone, so that none of the goddesses could have even the slightest idea, and none of them would be hurt in the slightest. . This is the real Advaita i.e. Dvaitadvaita, in which despite understanding duality well, a non-dual approach is adopted. Hence we can see that most of the people misunderstand Advaita.

This philosophy called Shavid also positively generates interest in Vedic-mythological subjects. People follow the Puranas occasionally, especially when some special religious event is going on, like the weekly Puranayagya etc. No one gets non-dual benefits from the Puranas by reading it every day. For this reason, there does not appear to be any special spiritual progress, but the same spiritual level remains. However, those who read and listen to the Puranas daily, their non-duality always remains present. Occasional week long Puranayagyas provide inspiration to read the Puranas daily. Therefore, to keep the society healthy in every way, weeklong Puranayagya should be held. Shavid appears to be even more non-dual than the Puranas, because its contemplation and following itself takes place continuously, the reason for which is its constant presence in our own body; that is why it is never forgotten. In the end, a mixed use of both seems to be the best, because according to 'Yatpinde Tatbrahmande' means 'what is there in body, the same is there in the universe', all the objects and meanings of the Puranas are imposed on the body of the reader, due to which the best kind of non-dual perspective is always maintained in life. One thing this philosophy teaches is that without human nature, non-attachment or non-duality does not have much practical importance. This tells us that just like the subtle physical body-being, maintaining non-duality even amidst humanistic tendencies is most fruitful and most beautiful, most fruitful and most beautiful.

Thank you for reading this book.

Good luck.

Do not forget its second part, 'Mythical body' in which Shavid means Sharirvigyan darshan is beautifully described. Both books are also available in the Audio format.

Other books written and recommended by Premyogi Vajra~

1) Love story of a Yogi- what Patanjali says

2) Kundalini demystified- what Premyogi vajra says

3) Kundalini Science – A Spiritual Psychology

4) The art of self-publishing and website creation

6) Kundalini demystified – What does Premyogi Vajra say?

7) Organic planet– the autobiography of an eco-loving Yogi

8) My Kundalini website on e-reader

9) My kundalini website on e-reader

10) Physiology or Philosophy - A Modern Kundalini Tantra (A Yogi's Love Story)

11) Kundalini science~a spiritual psychology (book-1,2,3 and 4)

12) Blackhole doing Yoga

13) Yoga in quantum science and space science

14) Purana riddle

15) Mythological body- a new age physiological philosophy (second part of the present book)

16) Comic mythology

All these above books are also available in Audiobook format.

The description of these books is also available on the webpage "Shop (Library)" of his personal website https://demystifyingkundalini.com/shop/. Please follow/subscribe to this website, "https://demystifyingkundalini.com/" for free to get new posts (especially Kundalini related) on a weekly basis and stay in regular touch.

Good luck everywhere.